The Saintly McCheyne

Robert Murray McCheyne was born at 14 Dublin Street, Edinburgh, on 21st May 1813, the youngest of a family of three sons and two daughters. His father Adam, was a lawyer and later became a Writer to the Signet.

When he was 18 years of age, his oldest brother, David, who had shown an earnest interest in his salvation, became ill and died, and this made a deep impression on him. When writing to one of his flock some years later he said: 'This day eleven years ago, I lost my loved and loving brother, and so began to seek a Brother who cannot die.'

The experience of his conversion is given in the hymn he wrote entitled 'Jehovah Tsidkenu.'

When free grace awoke me, by light from on high
Then legal fears shook me I trembled to die.
No refuge, no safety in self could I see
Jehovah Tsidkenu my Saviour must be.

After a brilliant career at Edinburgh University he entered the Divinity Hall and studied under Dr. Thomas Chalmers. He was licensed to preach the Gospel by the Presbytery of Annan on 1st July 1835. That same year he became assistant to Rev. John Bonar at Larbert and Dunipace, where he laboured for eleven months. He was ordained to the ministry and inducted at St. Peters church in Dundee on 24th November 1836. Almost immediately there were tokens of blessing, but after only two years he became ill and during a period of enforced rest he was sent to Palestine on a mission of inquiry to the Jews. During his absence the congregation experienced a great revival and the blessings of this continued after he returned home.

It was while doing his pastoral visitation during an epidemic that he caught typhus fever and died on the 25th March 1843.

Perhaps the two most striking characteristics of his life were his personal holiness and his love for the lost. In a letter to another minister, he wrote 'It is not great talents God blesses so much as great likeness to Christ'. His constant prayer was 'Oh God, make me as holy as it is possible for a sinner saved by grace on this earth to be.'

His close personal friend, Dr. Andrew Bonar, sought to sum up the life of McCheyne in the following words:

'But there has been one among us who, ere he had reached the age at which a priest in Israel would have been entering his course, dwelt at the mercy seat as if it were his home, preached the certainties of eternal life with an undoubting mind, and spent his days and nights in ceaseless breathings after holiness and the salvation of sinners. Hundreds of souls were his reward from the Lord ere he left us; and in him have we been taught how one man may do, who will only press farther into the presence of His God, and handle more skilfully the unsearchable riches of Christ, and speak more boldly for his God.'

May the Holy Spirit speak to your heart as you read the writings of this choice servant of God.

Stanley Barnes
Hillsborough, Co. Down
October 1995

Dedicated to the memory of
VIOREL ISAC
and
EMMANUEL TAMAS
Romanian brothers now 'with Christ'

God Makes A Path

THROUGH THE YEAR
with
Robert Murray McCheyne

Compiled by
STANLEY BARNES

AMBASSADOR

Ambassador Productions Ltd.
Providence House
16 Hillview Avenue,
Belfast, BT5 6JR
Northern Ireland

Emerald House
1 Chick Springs Road, Suite 102
Greenville,
South Carolina 29609

January

> "
>
> *I cannot understand McCheyne;*
> *grace seems to be natural to him.*
>
> "
>
> DR. ROBERT CANDLISH

January *first*

Do not forget

.... the fashion of this world passeth away
I Corinthians 7 v 31

A believer stands on a watch tower - things present are below his feet - things eternal are before his eyes. A little while, brethren, and the day of grace will be over, preaching, praying will be done. Soon we shall give over wrestling with an unbelieving world - soon the number of believers shall be complete, and the sky open over our heads, and Christ shall come. His parting cry was: "Surely I come quickly." Then we shall see him "whom, having not seen, we loved." A little while, and we shall stand before the great white throne; a little while, and the wicked shall not be - we shall see them going away into everlasting punishment; a little while, and the work of eternity shall be begun. We shall be like him - we shall see him day and night in his temple - we shall sing the new song, without sin and without weariness, for ever and ever. In a little moment, brethren, all this shall be: "For a small moment have I hid my face from thee; but with everlasting mercies will I gather thee."

January *second*

Self dedication

One shall say that I am the Lord's ....
Isaiah 44 v 5

Oh! there is no greater joy than for a believing soul to give himself all to God. This has always been the way in times of refreshing. It was so at Pentecost. First they gave their own selves unto the Lord. It was so with Boston, and Doddridge, and Edwards, and all the holy men of old.

"I have this day been before God," says Edwards, "and have given myself -all that I am and have - to God; so that I am in no respect my own. I can challenge no right in myself - in this understanding, this will, these affections. Neither have I right to this body, or any of its members - no right to this tongue, these hands, these feet, these eyes, these ears. I have given myself clean away."

Oh! would that you knew the joy of giving yourself away. You cannot keep yourself. Oh! this day try and give all to Him. Lie in His hand.

Where lies the blame

.... brethren, pray for us .....
II Thessalonians 3 v 1

Prayer is more powerful than preaching. It is prayer that gives preaching all its power. I observe that some Christians are very ready to censure ministers, and to complain of their preaching, of their coldness, their unfaithfulness. God forbid that I should ever defend unfaithful preaching or coldness, or deadness, in the ambassador of Christ! May my right hand sooner forget its cunning! But I do say, Where lies the blame of unfaithfulness? Where, but in the want of faithful praying? Why, the very hands of Moses would have fallen down, had they not been held up by his faithful people. Come then ye wrestlers of God, ye that climb Jacob's ladder, ye that wrestle Jacob's wrestling - strive you with God, that He may fulfil His word.

Look beyond

For I will pour water on him that is thirsty, and floods
upon the dry ground: I will pour my spirit upon thy seed,
and my blessing upon thine offspring.
Isaiah 44 v 3

Learn to look beyond ministers for a work of grace. God has given much honour to his ministers: but not the pouring out of the Spirit. He keeps that in His own hand: "I will pour." "It is not by might , nor by power, but by my spirit, saith the Lord of hosts." Alas! we would have little hope, if it depended upon ministers; for where are our men of might now? God is able to do it today as He was at the day of Pentecost; but men are taken up with ministers and not with God. As long as you look to ministers, God cannot pour; for you would say it came from man. Ah! cease from man, whose breath is in his nostrils. One would think we would be humbled in the dust by this time. In how many parishes of Scotland has God raised up faithful men, who cease not day and night to warn every one with tears! And yet still the heavens are like brass, and the earth like iron. Why? Just because your eye is on man, and not on God, Oh! look off man to Him, and He will pour; and His shall be all the glory.

January *fifth*

Believers shall grow like willows

*And they shall spring up as among the grass, as willows
by the water courses.*
Isaiah 44 v 4

There is nothing more distressing in our day than the want of growth among the children of God. They do not seem to press forward, they do not seem to be running a race. When I compare this year with last year, alas! where is the difference? - the same weakness, the same coldness; nay, I fear, greater languor in divine things. How different when the Spirit is poured out! They shall be like willows. You have seen the willow, how it grows - ceases not day or night, ever growing, ever shooting out new branches. Cut it down - it springs again. Ah! so would you be, dear Christians, if there were a flood-time of the Spirit, a day of Pentecost.

January *sixth*

Little fruit!

*Ask of me, and I shall give thee the heathen for thine inheritance, and
the uttermost parts of the earth for thy possession.*
Psalm 2 v 8

Two farmers possessed two fields that lay next each other. The one had rich crops, the other very scanty ones. "How comes it," says the one to the other, "that your field bears so well, and mine so poorly, when my land is as good as yours?"

"Why neighbour," said the other, "the reason is this - you only sow your field, but I both sow mine and harrow in the seed." Just so, my dear friends, there is little fruit among Christians, because there is little harrowing in by prayer. I think I could name many Christians among you who do not know one another, and never pray one with another. What wonder there is little fruit!

Christ, the key to the Scriptures

*And beginning at Moses and all the prophets, he expounded unto
them in all the scriptures the things concerning himself.*
Luke 24 v 27

When you are reading a book in a dark room and find it difficult, you take it to a window to get more light. So take your Bible to Christ. I thirst for the knowledge of the word, but most of all of Jesus Himself, the true Word.

Bread upon the waters

*Cast thy bread upon the waters: for thou shalt
find it after many days.*
Ecclesiastes 11 v 1

The excellent John Flavel was minister of Dartmouth in England. One day he preached from these words: 'If any man love not the Lord Jesus Christ, let him be anathema maranatha.' The discourse was unusually solemn, particularly the explanation of the curse. At the conclusion, when Mr Flavel rose to pronounce the blessing, he paused, and said: 'How shall I bless this whole assembly, when every person in it who loves not the Lord Jesus is anathema maranatha?' The solemnity of this address deeply affected the audience.

In the congregation was a lad named Luke Short, about fifteen years old, a native of Dartmouth. Shortly after, he went to sea, and sailed to America, where he passed the rest of his life. His life was lengthened far beyond the usual term. When a hundred years old, he was able to work on his farm, and his mind was not at all impaired. He had lived all this time in carelessness and sin; he was a sinner a hundred years old, and ready to die accursed. One day, as he sat in his field, he busied himself in reflecting on his past life. He thought of the days of his youth. His memory fixed on Mr. Flavel's sermon, a considerable part of which he remembered. The earnestness of the minister, the truths spoken, the effect on the people, all came fresh to his mind. He felt that he had not loved the Lord Jesus; he feared the dreadful anathema; he was deeply convinced of sin, was brought to the blood of sprinkling. He lived to his one hundred and sixteenth year, giving every evidence of being born again. Ah! how faithful God is to His Word. He did let none of His words fall to the ground.

Be of good cheer, Christian mothers, who weep over your unawakened children. They may be going far from you, perhaps across the seas and you tremble for their souls. Remember God can reach them everywhere. A believing mother never prayed in vain. Be instant in prayer. God will not forget His Word. He will let none of His words fall to the ground.

January *ninth*

The revealer of Christ

He shall glorify me: for he shall receive of mine, and
shall shew it unto you.
John 16 v 14

Dear friends, has the Spirit glorified Christ to you? He is still the great revealer of Christ. He shines into our heart, to give us the light of the knowledge of the glory of God, in the face of Christ. Has he led you to the altar, to the Lamb of God, that taketh away the sin of the world? Has he clothed you in the high priest's garments? Has he brought you within the veil, to the mercy-seat? This is His delightful work. Oh! it is a sweet work to be the minister on earth that leads souls to Christ - that points, like John, and says: 'Behold the Lamb of God!' But O how infinitely more loving is that Holy Spirit of God to lead trembling souls to Jesus! Oh praise him that has done this for you. Oh love the Spirit of God. 'Thy Spirit is good: lead me to the land of uprightness.'

January *tenth*

The answer to your prayer

But whosoever drinketh of the water that I shall give him shall never
thirst; but the water that I shall give him shall be in him a well of
water springing up into everlasting life.
John 4 v 14

My dear friends, have you received the Holy Ghost, since you believed? It appears to me that few Christians realise this river flowing after them. Oh what inexpressible love and grace there is in this work of the Spirit. Is there any of you weak and faint, and ready to perish under a wicked heart, and raging lusts? Or , have you got a thorn in the flesh, a messenger of Satan to buffet you, and you are driven to pray that it may be taken from you? See here the answer to your prayer. A river of living water flows from Christ. There is enough here for all your wants: 'My grace is sufficient for thee; for my strength is made perfect in weakness.' Some of you are afraid of the future; you fear some approaching temptation, you fear some coming contest. See here the river flows after you - the Spirit will abide with you for ever. Oh what love is here. Notwithstanding all your sinfulness, weakness and unbelief, still he abides with you, and will for ever. He is 'a well of water springing up into everlasting life' (John 4 v.14)

The victory of the blood

And they overcame him by the blood of the Lamb ...
Revelation 12 v11

We wrestle not with flesh and blood . An awakened soul often has an awful warfare with Satan. Satan fights against him in two ways: first, by stirring up his corruption's, and making his lusts to flame and burn within him in a fearful manner. Second, by accusing him. Satan is the accuser of the brethren. He accuses him in his conscience, in order to drive him away from Christ - to drive him to despair, and to give up all hope of salvation. He says to him: 'Thou art a vile wretch, not fit for a holy Saviour. See what raging lusts are in thy heart. Thou wilt never be saved.' Ah, when the poor sinner runs into Christ, he finds rest there - his warfare is then accomplished. He sees all the accusations of Satan answered in the blood of the Lamb.

When the soul faints

And ye have forgotten the exhortation which speaketh unto you as
unto children, My son, despise not thou the chastening of the Lord,
nor faint when thou art rebuked of him: For whom the Lord loveth he
chasteneth, and scourgeth every son whom he receiveth.
Hebrews 12 vs 5 & 6

Ah! it is a sad thing when the soul faints under the rebukes of God. They were intended to lead you deeper into Christ, into a fuller enjoyment of God. Faint not when thou art rebuked of Him. When a soul comes to Christ, he expects to be led to heaven in a green, soft pathway, without a thorn. On the contrary, he is led into darkness. Poverty stares him in the face, or bereavement writes him childless, or persecutions embitter his life; and now his soul remembers the wormwood and the gall. He forgets the love and wisdom that are dealing with him; he says: "I am the man that hath seen affliction. The Lord hath forsaken me, and my God hath forgotten me."

January *thirteenth*

Infinite love

He that loveth not knoweth not God; for God is love.
I John 4 v 8

A mother's love is the fullest love which we have on earth. She loves with all her heart. But there is no love more full than that of God toward his Son; God loves Jesus fully. The whole heart of the Father is, as it were, continually poured down in love upon the Lord Jesus. There is nothing in Christ that does not draw the infinite love of God. In Him God sees his own image perfectly, his own law acted out, his own will done. The Father loves the Son fully; but when a soul comes into Christ, the same love rests on that soul: 'That the love wherewith thou hast loved me may be in them' (John 17 v. 26).

January *fourteenth*

Unchanging love

*... having loved his own which were in the world,
he loved them unto the end.*
John 13 v 1

A mother's love is, of all creature-love, the most unchangeable. A boy leaves his parent's roof, he crosses a thousand seas, he labours beneath a foreign sky; he comes back, he finds his aged mother changed, her head is grey, her venerable brow is furrowed with age; still he feels while she clasps him to her bosom, that her heart is the same. But ah! far more unchanging is the love of God to Christ, and to a soul in Christ: 'I am the Lord; I change not.' The Father that loves has no variableness. Jesus, who is loved, is the same yesterday, today, and for ever. How can that love change? It flowed before the world was; it will flow when the world has passed away.

If you are in Christ, that love shines on you: 'I have loved thee with an everlasting love.' 'I am persuaded, that neither death, nor life, nor angels, nor principalities, nor powers, nor things present, not things to come, nor height, nor depth, nor any other creature, shall be able to separate us from the love of God, which is in Christ Jesus our Lord.'

January *fifteenth*

Be fervent in praise
By him therefore let us offer the sacrifice of praise to God
continually, that is, the fruit of our lips giving thanks to his name.
Hebrews 13 v 15

And, oh! be fervent in praise. Lift up your voices in it. Lift up your hearts in it. In heaven they wax louder and louder. John heard the sound of a great multitude; and then it was like many waters, and then it was like mighty thunderings, crying: 'Hallelujah! Hallelujah!' I remember Edwards' remark, that it was in the singing of praises that his people felt themselves most enlarged, and that then God was worshipped somewhat in the beauty of holiness.

Let it be so among yourselves. Learn, dearly beloved, to praise God heartily, to sing with all your heart and soul in the family and in the congregation. But, oh! remember that even your praises must be sprinkled with blood, and can be acceptable to God only by Jesus Christ.

January *sixteenth*

A lesson from the sun
... among whom ye shine as lights in the world;
Philippians 2 v 15

It is quite right to help the heathen at home, but it is just as right to help the heathen abroad. Oh that God would free you from a narrow mind, and give you his own divine Spirit. Learn a lesson from the sun. It shines both far and near; it does not pour its beams all into one sunny valley, or on one bright land. No, it journeys on from shore to shore, pours its rich beams upon the wide ocean, on the torrid sands of Africa, and the icy coasts of Greenland. Go you and do likewise. Shine as lights in the world.

January *seventeenth*

David's prayer

Open thou mine eyes, that I may behold wondrous
things out of thy law.
Psalm 119 v 18

Are there not some who read the Bible, but get little from it? You feel that it does not sink into your heart, it does not remain with you through the week, It is like the seed cast in the wayside, easily plucked away. Oh, it is just such an outpoured Spirit you require, to hide the Word in your heart. When you write with a dry pen, without any ink in it, no impression is made upon the paper. Now, ministers are the pens, and the Spirit of God is the ink. Pray that the pen may be filled with that living ink, that the Word may remain in your heart, known and read of all men, that you may be sanctified through the truth.

January *eighteenth*

When heaven came down

So that the priests could not stand to minister by reason of
the cloud: for the glory of the Lord had filled the house of God.
II Chronicles 5 v 14

Before the cloud came down, no doubt the priests were all busily engaged burning incense and offering sacrifices; but when the cloud came down, they could only wonder and adore. So it ever will be when the Lord gives much of his Spirit; He will make it evident that it is not the work of man.

If He were to give only a little then ministers would begin to think they had some hand in it; but when He fills the house, then He makes it plain that man has nothing to do with it. David Brainerd said, that when

God awakened his whole congregation of Indians, he stood by amazed, and felt that he was as nothing - that God alone was working.

Oh, it is this, dear friends, that we desire and pray for - that the Lord the Spirit would himself descend, and with His almighty power tear away the veil from your hearts, convincing you of sin, of righteousness, and of judgement; that Jesus Himself would take His sceptre and break your hard hearts, and take all the glory, that we may cry out: 'Not unto us. Lord, not unto us, but unto Thy name give glory.'

January *nineteenth*

Asked to a feast

I am the living bread which cometh down from heaven: if any man eat of this bread, he shall live for ever and the bread that I will give is my flesh, which I will give for the life of the world.
John 6 v 51

Christians, learn to feed more on Christ: 'Eat, O friends! drink, yea drink abundantly, O beloved!' When you are asked to a feast, there is no greater affront you can put upon the entertainer than by being content with a crumb below the table. Yet this is the way the Christians of our day affront the Lord of glory. Oh, how few seem to feed much on Christ! How few seem to put on his white flowing raiment! How few seem to drink deep into his Spirit! Most are content with a glimpse now and then of pardon - a crumb from the table, and a drop of his Spirit. Awake, dear friends! 'These things have I spoken unto you, that your joy may be full.'

January *twentieth*

The grand object

That he might present it to himself a glorious church, not having spot, or wrinkle, or any such thing; but that it should be holy and without blemish.
Ephesians 5 v 27

Some are afraid they will never be holy: 'I shall fall under my sin' You shall be made holy. It was for this Christ died. This was the grand object he had in view. This was what was in his eye - to build a holy Church out of a world of lost sinners; to pluck brands out of the fire and make them trees of righteousness; to choose poor, black souls, and make them fair brothers and sisters round his throne. Christ will not lose this object.

Look up, then - be not afraid. He redeemed you to make you holy. Though you had a million of worlds opposing you, he will do it: 'He is faithful, who also will do it.'

January *twenty-first*

A threefold grace

For ye know the grace of our Lord Jesus Christ, that, though
he was rich, yet for your sakes he became poor, that ye through
his poverty might be rich.
2 Corinthians 8 v 9

When Jesus washed the disciples' feet, when he came to Peter, Peter said, ' Lord, dost thou wash my feet?' Three things amazed him:

(1) The glorious being that knelt down before him: 'Thou'.
(2) The lowly action he was going to perform: 'Dost thou wash?'
(3) The vile wretch whose feet were to be washed: 'My feet'. He was amazed at the grace of the Lord Jesus.

So in this amazing work you may see a threefold grace:
(1) The glorious being that undertook for sinners: 'He who was rich'.
(2) The depth to which he stooped: He became poor.'
(3) The wretches whose souls were to be washed: 'For your sakes'. Ah! well may you be amazed this day, and cry out: 'Dost thou wash my soul?'

January *twenty-second*

The true smitten rock

In the last day , that great day of the feast, Jesus stood and cried,
saying If any man thirst, let him come unto me, and drink.
John 7 v 37

The feast of the tabernacles was intended to be a picture of the time when the fathers of the Jewish nation lived in tents in the wilderness. It was intended to remind them that they too were strangers and pilgrims in the wilderness, and that they were journeying to a better land. But there was one thing in the wilderness which they had no resemblance of in the feast of tabernacles - the smitten rock which gave out rivers of water. In order to make up for this deficiency, it is said that on the last day of the feast of the Jews used to draw water in a golden pitcher from the Fountain of Siloam, and pour it out upon the morning sacrifice, as it lay upon the altar. They did this great rejoicing, having palm branches in their hands, and singing the twelfth chapters of Isaiah. Now it was on this very day, perhaps at that very time, that Jesus stood up in the midst of them, and, as if he wished to show them that he was the true smitten rock, cried: 'If any man thirst, let him come unto me and drink.'

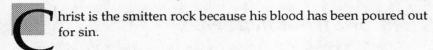

January *twenty-third*

Rivers of water

And Moses lifted up his hand, and with his rod he smote the rock twice and the water came out abundantly, and the congregation drank, and their beast also.
Numbers 20 v 11

Christ is the smitten rock because his blood has been poured out for sin.

(1) The rock was smitten before it gave out the stream. So is it with Christ. He was smitten of God and afflicted. He bore the wrath of God; and therefore his blood gushed forth, and cleanses from all sin. Oh! you that fear to be smitten of God, wash in this blood, - it flows from a smitten rock.

(2) The water gushed forth abundantly when Moses smote the rock. It was no scanty stream - it was enough for all the thousands of Israel. So is it with the blood of the Saviour. It is no scanty stream. There are no sins it cannot wash out, there is no sinner beyond its reach, there is enough here for all the thousands of Israel.

(3) It was a constant supply: 'They drank of the spiritual rock which followed them, and that rock was Christ.' We are not expressly told in the Old Testament that the waters of the smitten rock did actually follow the camp of Israel, but some learned divines are of the opinion that it was so - that the water continued to flow wherever Israel went; so that it might be said the smitten rock followed them. So it is with Christ. He is a rock that follows us. He is like rivers of water in a dry place. You may wash, and wash again.

January *twenty-fourth*

Fruitful to the last

*The righteous shall flourish like the palm tree; he shall grow like a
cedar in Lebanon. Those that be planted in the house of the Lord shall
flourish in the courts of our God. They shall still bring forth fruit in
old age; they shall be fat and flourishing.*
Psalm 92 v 12 -14

The palm tree and cedar have both this wonderful property, that
they are fruitful to the last: and so it is with the living believer -
he is a Christian to the last - full of the Spirit, full of love, full of
holiness to the last. Like fine wine, the older the better. 'The path of the
just is like the shining light, which shineth more and more unto the perfect day.'

January *twenty-fifth*

The Lord from heaven

*The first man is of the earth, earthy: the second man is the
Lord from heaven.*
I Corinthians 15 v 47

The first Adam was fair, exquisitely fair, as he came from the hand
of God; but the second is altogether lovely - fairer than the children of men.

The first Adam was made in the likeness of God; but the second is
God Himself, the Lord from heaven - the brightness of the Father's glory,
and the express image of His person.

The first Adam was full of heavenly wisdom, so that he named all the
creatures as they came; but in the second are hid all the treasures of
wisdom and knowledge. He is the wisdom of God. He spake as never
man spake. He calls all the stars by their names.

The first was the head of the whole human race - the federal head; so
that in him they stood, and in him they fell. Christ is offered as a head to
every creature, and is actually the head of all the redeemed, and of myri-
ads of holy angels, all gathered together in him.

O glorious one! Divine and human perfections meet in Him! O that
you were filled with sweet, admiring, adoring thoughts of Him this day!
O that He would rise upon you like the sun! He is the Light of the

world, the Sun of righteousness, the bright and morning Star. It is that one who justifies the ungodly, who has power to forgive sins. He is precious to all that believe.

Something better than life

For to me to live is Christ, and to die is gain.
Philippians 1 v 21

If you would die the death of Christ's people, you must live their life. Inconsistent Christians generally have a painful death-bed; but those that follow Christ fully can die like aged Paul - 'I am ready to be offered'; or like Job - 'I know that my Redeemer liveth.'

Following Jesus

Jesus saith unto him, If I will that he tarry till I come, what is that to thee? follow thou me.
John 21 v 22

If you would follow Christ fully, you must know Him fully. A sight of His beauty draws us to follow Him. 'He is the chief among ten thousand, and altogether lovely.' 'And I, if I be lifted up, will draw all men unto me.; There is an indescribable loveliness in Christ that draws the soul to follow Him. All divine perfections dwell in Him; and yet He offers to save us.

His suitableness draws us to follow Him. He just answers the need of our soul. We are all guilty, he is all righteousness. We, all weakness; He, all strength. Nothing can more completely answer our soul than Christ doth. The chickens run under the feathers of their mother when they see them stretched out, the dove flutters into the clefts, Noah into the ark; and our soul thus follows Jesus.

His freeness draws us to follow Him. 'He will in no wise cast out.' He forgives seventy times seven. It is the keeping the eye on Christ that makes you follow Him. It is seeing the King in His beauty that makes the soul cleave to him, and run after Him. 'My soul followeth hard after thee.' 'Run the race set before you, looking unto Jesus.'

January *twenty-eighth*

Eternal loss

For we must all appear before the judgment seat of Christ; that
every one may receive the things done in his body, according to that
he hath done, whether it be good or bad.
II Corinthians 5 v 10

Every man shall be rewarded according as his work has been. Some will be made rulers over five, some over ten cities. I have no doubt that every sin, inconsistency, backsliding and decay of God's children takes away something from their eternal glory. It is a loss for all eternity; and the more fully and unreservedly we follow the Lord Jesus now, the more abundant will our entrance be into His everlasting kingdom. The closer we walk with Christ now, the closer will we walk with Him to all eternity. 'Thou hast a few names in Sardis which have not defiled their garments. They shall walk with me in white, for they are worthy.' Amen.

January *twenty-ninth*

To be like Jesus

For whom he did foreknow, he also did predestinate to be
conformed to the image of his Son, that he might be the first born
among many brethren.
Romans 8 v 29

But we all, with open face beholding as in a glass the glory of the Lord, are changed into the same image from glory to glory, even as by the Spirit of the Lord. (II Corinthians 3 v.18).

Our foolish hearts think it better to retain some part of Satan's image, but, ah! this is our happiness, to reflect every feature of Jesus, and that for ever. To have no inconsistency, to be like Him in every part; to love like Him, to weep like Him, to pray like Him, to be changed into His likeness: 'I shall be satisfied when I awake with Thy likeness.'

Victory assured

These things I have spoken unto you, that in me ye might have peace. In the world ye shall have tribulation: but be of good cheer; I have overcome the world.
John 16 v 33

In all other battles we do not know how the victory is to turn until the battle is won. In the battle of Waterloo, it was long thought that the French had gained; and Napoleon sent several despatches to Paris telling that he had won. But in the fight with the world, Satan and the flesh, we know how the victory is to turn already. Christ has engaged to carry us through. He will guard us against the darts of the law, by hiding us in His blood, He defends us from the power of sin by His Holy Spirit put within us. He will keep us, in the secret of His presence, from the strife of tongues. The thicker the battle, the closer will He keep to us; so that we can sing already: 'I thank God, through Jesus Christ our Lord.' We know that we shall overcome. Though the world were a million times more enraged - though the fires of persecution were again to be kindled - though my heart were a million times more wicked - though all the temptations of hell were let loose upon me - I know I shall overcome through Him that loved me. When Paul and Silas sang in the low dungeon, they were more than conquerors. When Paul sang, in spite of his thorn, 'I will glory in my infirmities,' he was more than a conqueror.

The work of Christ

The Lord is well pleased for his righteousness' sake; he will magnify the law, and make it honourable.
Isaiah 42 v.21

This is in some respects the most wonderful description of the work of Christ given in the whole Bible. He is often said to have ful filled the law. Thus, Matthew 3 v.15: 'Thus it becometh us to fulfil all righteousness.' And again, Matthew 5 v 17: ' Think not that I am come to destroy the law, or the prophets: I am not come to destroy, but to fulfil.' But here it is said, He will 'magnify the law, and make it honourable.; He came to give new lustre and glory to the holy law of God, that all worlds might see and understand that the law is holy, and just, and good. When God wrote the law upon the heart of Adam in His creation, that was magnifying the law. He showed it to a be great and holy and happy law, when he wrote it in the bosom of so holy and happy a creature as man then was. When God spoke the law from Mount Sinai, that magnified the law, and made it glorious. When He spoke it with His own voice in so dreadful a manner, when He wrote it twice with His own finger, this was magnifying it - enough, one would think, to make our modern Sabbath breakers tremble to erase it. But most of all when Christ died, did He give lustre, and greatness, and glory, and majesty, to the law of God in the sight of all worlds.

Robert Murray McCheyne's Vestry

February

> **"**
>
> *My recollections of McCheyne are those of a tall slender lad, with a sweet pleasant face, bright yet grave, fond of play and of a blameless life.*
>
> **"**
>
> CHARLES DENT BELL
> RECTOR OF CHELTENHAM

February *first*

The love of Christ

And to know the love of Christ, which passeth knowledge, that ye
might be filled with all the fulness of God.
Ephesians 3 v 19

Paul says: 'The love of Christ passeth knowledge.' It is like the blue sky, into which you may see clearly, but the real vastness of which you cannot measure. It is like the deep, deep sea, into whose bosom you can look a little way, but its depths are unfathomable. It has a breadth without a bound, length without end, height without top, and depth without bottom. If holy Paul said this, who was so deeply taught in divine things, who had been in the third heaven and seen the glorified face of Jesus, how much more may we, poor and weak believers, look into that love and say: It passeth knowledge!

February *second*

Face to face

And they shall see his face; and his name shall be in
their foreheads.
Revelation 22 v 4

Mark the perfect man, and behold the upright; for the end of that man is peace. God calls upon you to mark the death-bed of His children. Sometimes it is triumphant, like Stephen: 'Behold, I see the heavens opened, and the Son of Man standing at the right hand of God. Lord Jesus, receive my spirit.' Almost always peaceful - or, if it be that the sun goes down in a cloud, O how sweet the surprise, when the believer finds himself on the other side of Jordan, at the pearly; gate of the New Jerusalem, in the arms of the angels, in the smile of Jesus! 'There is a rest remaining for the people of God.'

O happy believer

... and whoso trusteth in the Lord, happy is he.
Proverbs 16 v 20

Become one with Christ, and even this moment you are lovely in the sight of God - comely, through His comeliness put upon you. You are as much accepted in the sight of God as is the Son of Man, the Beloved that sits on His right hand. The Spirit shall be given you, as surely as He is given to Christ. He is given to Christ as the oil of gladness, wherewith he is anointed above his fellows. You are as sure to wear a crown of glory, as that Christ is now wearing His. You are as sure to sit upon Christ's throne, as that Christ is now sitting on His Father's throne. O weep for joy, happy believer! O sing for gladness of heart: 'For I am persuaded that neither death, nor life, nor angels, nor principalities, nor powers nor things present, nor things to come, nor height, nor depth, nor any other creature, shall be able to separate us from the love of God, which is in Christ Jesus our Lord.'

A peculiar people

Wherefore come out from among them, and be ye separate,
saith the Lord ...
II Corinthians 6 v 17

Ephraim, he hath mixed himself among the people (Hosea 7 v. 8). This was the peculiar character of the Jews: 'The people shall dwell alone, and shall not be reckoned among the nations.' But when they mixed themselves among the nations, then grey hairs began to appear. So it is with Christians, they are a peculiar people. Jesus said of them: 'They are not of the world, even as I am not of the world.' We are as completely separated from the world as Christ was; we have got his blood upon us, and the Holy Spirit in us; we have peculiar joys and peculiar sorrows; we are a praying people, a praising people. But the moment we begin to mix with the ungodly, grey hairs begin to appear - our souls wither.

February *fifth*

A constant appetite

This book of the law shall not depart out of thy mouth; but thou shalt meditate therein day and night, that thou mayest observe to do according to all that is written therein: for then thou shalt make thy way prosperous, and then thou shalt have good success.
Joshua 1 v 8

When a soul is first brought to Christ, he delights in the Word of God. He has an appetite for it 'as a new-born babe'. Just as an infant has a constant, steadily-recurring appetite for its mother's milk, so has the soul for the Word. He has spiritual understanding of the Word. It seems all sweet and easy. It all testifies of Jesus. The soul grasps the meaning or earnestly inquires from ministers and others the meaning of difficult passages. He has growth: 'That ye may grow thereby.' It is felt to be the daily nourishment of the soul, the sword to ward off temptation.

How different when the Christian is in decay! No relish for the Word. It may be read as a duty, or as a burdensome task but it is not delighted in. Other books are preferred to the Bible. There is no growing in the knowledge of the Word, no self-application, no receiving it with meekness, no frequent recurrence of the mind during the day to the chapter read in the morning, no answering Satan by 'Thus it is written' and 'Thus saith the Lord'. Ah! my friends, how is the gold become dim!

'...yea gray hairs are here and there upon him, yet he knoweth not.' (Hosea 7 v. 9)

February *sixth*

Growing days

If thou turn away thy foot from the sabbath, from doing thy pleasure on my holy day; and call the sabbath a delight, the holy of the Lord, honourable; and shalt honour him, not doing thine own ways, nor finding thine own pleasure, nor speaking thine own words: Then shalt thou delight thyself in the Lord.
Isaiah 58 v 13 & 14

There was a time when Sabbath days were growing days. Hungry souls came to the Word, and went away filled with good things. They came like Martha, and went away like Mary. They came like Samson, when his locks were shorn, and went away like Samson when his locks were grown.

Soul thirst

As the hart panteth after the water brooks, so panteth my soul after thee, O God.
Psalm 42 v 1

These are supposed to be the words of David when he fled from his son Absalom. He seems to have been wandering in some solitary wild on the side of Mount Hermon, the stream of Jordan flowing at his feet. David seems to have been full of pensive meditation: for his enemies reproached him daily, saying: 'Where is thy God?' nay, even God seemed to forget him, all his waves and billows were going over him; when suddenly a deer bounded past him. It had been sore wounded by the archers, or pursued by some wild beast on the mountains of the leopards. Faint and weary, he saw it rushing towards the flowing stream, and quenching its thirst in the water brook. His soul was quickened by the sight. Is not this just a picture of what I should be? Is not my God all to me that the flowing stream is to that wounded deer? 'As the hart panteth after the water brooks, so panteth my soul after thee, O God.'

More blessed to give

... It is more blessed to give than to receive.
Acts 20 v 35

These words form part of a most touching address which Paul made to the elders of Ephesus, when he parted with them for the last time. He took them all to witness that He was pure from the blood of all men: 'For I have not shunned to declare unto you all the counsel of God.' It is deeply interesting to notice that the duty of giving to the poor is marked by Him as one part of the counsel of God; so much so, that He makes it His last word to them: 'I have showed you all things, how that so labouring ye ought to support the weak, and to remember the words of the Lord Jesus, how He said, It is more blessed to give than to receive.' These words, which he quotes from the mouth of the

Saviour, are nowhere to be found in the Gospels. It is the only traditional saying of our Lord that has been preserved. It seems to have been one of his household words, a common-place, uttered by Him again and again: 'It is more blessed to give than to receive.'

February *ninth*

Where you are

.... and to every man his work ...
Mark 13 v 34

L earn, my dear friends, to keep to your own work. When the Lord has hung up a lamp in one corner, is there no presumption in removing it to another? Is not the Lord wiser than man? Every one of you have your work to do for Christ where you are. Are you on a sick-bed? Still you have your work to do for Christ there as much as the highest servant of Christ in the world. The smallest twinkling star is as much a servant of God as the mid-day sun. Only live for Christ where you are.

February *tenth*

He's preparing a place

In my Father's house are many mansions: if it were not so, I would have told you. I go to a prepare a place for you.
John 14 v 2

W hen a family are going to emigrate to a foreign shore, often the elder brother goes before to prepare a place for his younger brethren. This is what Christ has done. He does not intend that we should live here always - He has gone a far journey in order to prepare a place for us: 'I go to prepare a place for you; and if I go and prepare a place for you, I will come again and receive you unto myself; that where I am, there ye may be also.' Oh, Christians! believe in Christ preparing a place for you. It will greatly take away the fear of dying. It is an awful thing to die, even for a forgiven and sanctified soul to enter on a world unknown, unseen, untried. One thing takes away fear: Christ is preparing a place quite suitable for my soul. He knows all the wants and weaknesses of my frame. I know He will make it a pleasant home to me.

Give liberally

*... He which soweth sparingly shall reap also sparingly; and he
which soweth bountifully shall reap also bountifully.*
II Corinthians 9 v 6

I am going to say now what the world will scoff at. But all that I
ask of you is, to be like the Bereans. Search the Scriptures, and see
if these things be not so. The whole Bible shows, then, that the
best way to have plenty in this world is to give liberally. 'Cast thy bread
upon the waters, and thou shalt find it after many days.' This refers to
the sowing of rice. The rice in the East is always sown when the fields
are flooded with water. The bread-corn is actually cast upon the water.
After many days the waters dry up, and a rich crop of waving rice covers the plain. So it is in giving liberally to the poor out of love to Jesus. It
is like throwing away your money - it is like casting seed upon the waters. Yet fear not, you shall find a crop after many days - you shall have
a return for your money in this world.

Follow the Lord fully

*Hebron, therefore became the inheritance of Caleb the son of
Jephunneh the Kenezite unto this day, because that he wholly fol-
lowed the Lord God of Israel.*
Joshua 14 v 14

P ray to be made like Caleb, who had another spirit, and followed
the Lord fully. Follow Christ all the day. He is the continual burnt-
offering in whom you may have peace. He is the rock that follows you, from whom you may have constant and infinite supplies. Give
yourself wholly away to Him. You are safe in no other keeping but in
the everlasting arms of Jehovah Jesus.

February *thirteenth*

The spring of the soul

And I will pour upon the house of David, and upon the inhabitants of Jerusalem, the spirit of grace and of supplications: and they shall look upon me whom they have pierced, and they shall mourn for him, as one mourneth for his only son, and shall be in bitterness for him as one that is in bitterness for his first-born....In that day there shall be a fountain opened to the house of David and to the inhabitants of Jerusalem, for sin and for uncleanness.
Zechariah 12 v 10; 13 v 1

In these words you have a description of the conversion of the Jews, which is yet to come - an event that will give life to this dead world. But God's method is the same in the conversion of any soul. Conversion is the most glorious work of God. The creation of the sun is a very glorious work - when God first rolled him flaming along the sky, scattering out golden blessings on every shore. The change in spring is very wonderful - when God makes the faded grass revive, the dead trees put out green leaves, and the flowers appear on the earth. But far more glorious and wonderful is the conversion of a soul! It is the creation of a sun that is to shine for eternity; it is the spring of the soul that shall know no winter; the planting of a tree that shall bloom with eternal beauty in the paradise of God.

February *fourteenth*

Grace sufficient

And he said unto me, My grace is sufficient for thee: for my strength is made perfect in weakness. Most gladly therefore will I rather glory in my infirmities, that the power of Christ may rest upon me.
II Corinthians 12 v 9

When Paul was caught up into paradise he thought he would never again feel his body of sin; but when he was humbled and made to know himself better, and to know the grace that is in Christ, then his glory ever after was, that he had a weak body of sin and death, and that there was power enough in Christ to keep him from falling. From that day he gloried not that he had no sin in him, but that he had an almighty Saviour dwelling in him and upholding him. He took pleasure now in every thing that made him feel his weakness; for this drove him to Jesus for strength.

Learn, dear brethren, the true glory of a Christian in this world. The world knows nothing of it. A true Christian has a body of sin . He has every lust and corruption that is in the heart of man or devil. He wants no tendency to sin. If the Lord has given you light, you know and feel this. What is the difference, then, between you and the world? Infinite! You are in the hand of Christ. His Spirit is within you. He is able to keep you from falling.; 'Rejoice in the Lord, ye righteous; and shout for joy all ye that are upright in heart.'

Do not doubt

Now Jesus loved...Lazarus.
John 11 v 5

Christ loved Lazarus peculiarly, and yet he afflicted him very sore. A surgeon never bends his eye so tenderly upon his patient, as when he is putting in the lancet, or probing the wound to the very bottom. And so with Christ; He bends His eye most tenderly over His own at the time He is afflicting them.

Do not doubt the holy love of Jesus to your soul when he is laying a heavy hand upon you. Jesus did not love Lazarus less when he afflicted him, but rather more - even as a father correcteth a son in whom he delighteth (Proverbs 3 v. 12). A goldsmith when he casts gold into the furnace looks after it.

Radiant saints

Ye are the light of the world. A city that is set
on an hill cannot be hid.
Matthew 5 v 14

If the sun were to grow weary of running his daily journey, and were to give over shining, would you not say it should be taken down, for did not God hang it in the sky to give light upon the earth? Just so, dear Christians, if you grow weary in well-doing, in shining with Christ's beauty, in walking by Christ's Spirit, you, too, should be taken down and cast away - for did not Christ arise upon you for this very end, that you might be a light in the world? Ah! think of this, dark, useless Christians, who are putting your candle under a bushel. I tremble for some who will not lay themselves out for Christ. Ah! you are wronging yourselves and dishonouring Christ. Your truest happiness is in shining; the more you shine for Christ, the happier you will be. 'To me to live is Christ; and to die, gain.'

February *seventeenth*

A day's march nearer home

But the path of the just is as the shining light, that shineth more and more unto the perfect day.
Proverbs 4 v 18

When Israel was travelling the wilderness they came nearer to the good land every step they took. They had a long wilderness to pass through, still every day's journey brought them nearer to the end. So it is with all that are in Christ Jesus. Every step is bringing them nearer to heaven. Every day they are coming nearer and nearer to glory. 'Now it is high time to awake out of sleep; for now is our salvation nearer than when we believed'. 'The night is far spent, the day is at hand.' Every soul that is carried on the wings of the eagle is flying towards the rest that remaineth. The hours fly fast; but as fast flies that divine eagle. In running a race, every step brings you nearer to the end of it, nearer to the prize, to the crown.

February *eighteenth*

Delays are not denials

When Jesus heard that, he said, This sickness is not unto death, but for the glory of God, that the Son of God might be glorified thereby.
John 11 v 4

When we ask for something agreeable to God's will, and in the name of Christ, we know that we have the petitions which we desire of Him. But the time, He keeps in His own power. God is very sovereign in the time of His answers. When Martha and Mary sent their petition to Christ, He gave them an immediate promise; but the answer was not when they expected. So Christ frequently gives us the desires of our heart, though not at the peculiar time we desired, but a better time. Do not be weary in putting up prayers, say for the conversion of a friend. They may be answered when you are in the dust. Hold on to pray. He will answer in the best time. 'Be not weary in well-doing; for in due season we shall reap, if we faint not.'

Persecution

Yea, and all that will live godly in Christ Jesus shall
suffer persecution.
II Timothy 3 v 12

T he history of the Church in all ages has been a history of perse-cution. No sooner does a soul begin to show concern for religion, no sooner does that soul cleave to Jesus, than the world talk, to the grief of those whom God hath wounded. What bitter words are hurled against that soul! In all ages this has been true: 'They wandered about in sheep-skins and goat-skins, being destitute, afflicted, tormented; of whom the world was not worthy.' Those that eat the bread of God have often been driven from their quiet meal - those who are clothed with Christ have often had to part with worldly clothing, and have been exposed to famine, nakedness, peril and sword - the last extremity. Cain murdered Abel. They killed the Prince of Life; and so all his creatures ever since have been exposed to the same.

Giving Him the glory

... to him be glory and dominion for ever and ever. Amen.
Revelation 1 v 6

T he saved soul longs to give glory to Christ. He looks back over all the way by which he has been led, and says from the bottom of his heart, To him be glory. He looks to the love of Jesus - to his awakening, drawing, washing, renewing, making a king and priest. Min-isters may have been used as instruments, but he looks far beyond these and says, To him be glory. A true Christian will cast his crown no where but at the feet of Jesus. It was He that loved me, He that washed me. - To him be glory.

February *twenty-first*

Amazing love

... the Son of God, who loved me, and gave himself for me.
Galatians 2 v 20

When Jacob loved Rachel, he served seven years for her - he bore the summer's heat and winter's cold. But Jesus bore the hot wrath of God, and the winter blast of His Father's anger, for those He loved. Jonathan loved David with more than the love of women, and for his sake he bore the cruel anger of his father, Saul. But Jesus, out of love to us, bore the wrath of His Father poured out without mixture. It was the love of Christ that made Him leave the love of His Father, the adoration of angels, and the throne of glory. It was love that made Him not despise the Virgin's womb; it was love that made Him hungry and thirsty and weary; love made Him hasten to Jerusalem; love led Him to gloomy, dark Gethsemane; love bound and dragged Him to the judgement hall; love nailed Him to the cross; love bowed His head beneath the amazing load of His Father's anger. 'Greater love hath no man than this.' 'I am the good Shepherd; the good Shepherd giveth his life for the sheep.'

February *twenty-second*

Sweet companionship

... thy people shall be my people, and thy God my God:
Ruth 1 v 16

The soul in Christ has many sweet companions - brothers and sisters in Christ Jesus. The soul that is united to the Vine-tree is united to all the branches: 'We know that we are passed from death unto life, because we love the brethren.' 'I am a companion of all them that fear thee.'

Believers have many things to say to one another; as John says to Gaius: 'I had many things to write unto thee, but I will not with ink and pen write unto thee: but I trust I shall shortly see thee, and we shall speak face to face;' So did believers in the days of Malachi: 'Then they that feared the Lord spake often one to another: and the Lord hearkened, and heard..' (Malachi 3 v.16). And so do believers still. They may tell of their past experiences modestly, humbly, with self-loathing, and for the glory of Christ; as Jesus told the maniac: 'Return to thine own house, and show how great things God hath done unto thee' (Luke 8 v.39); and as David speaks: 'Come and hear, all ye that fear God, and I will declare what he hath done for my soul' (Psalm 66 v.16).

February *twenty-third*

Before and after

What? know ye not that your body is the temple of the Holy Ghost
which is in you, which ye have of God, and ye are not your own.
I Corinthians 6 v 19

A saved soul gives himself away to Christ for ever. Before conversion a man loves to be his own master, to do what he will with his time, his money, his influence, his all. But when Jesus lays His hand on him, washes and renews him, then he says, 'I am the Lord's . I am not my own, but bought with a price.

February *twenty-fourth*

Something to give

My son, give me thine heart, and let thine eyes observe my ways.
Proverbs 23 v 26

Oh Christians, come and give up your all to Christ - give up your heart to Him. Let His dominion be from sea to sea in your heart - from one corner to another. Is there any part of your heart where you do not wish Christ to reign. Then you have not seen Him, neither known Him. Give up your all to Him. Your dearest friends. Say, they are not mine, but Christ's; and so you will part from them, not without a tear, but without losing your all. If there is any thing you are unwilling Christ should have, then you are not His. Oh, it is sweet to have nothing our own, but to give up all to Christ - to be entirely His for ever and ever. Once you gave all to Satan. Now give all to Christ.

February *twenty-fifth*

Riches untold

That in everything ye are enriched by him ...
I Corinthians 1 v 5

Kings in olden time had immense possessions. Of one it is said, 'the sun never set on his dominions.' Solomon gathered all the peculiar treasures of kings. But a soul united to Jesus has more. He has got the pearl of great price, the clothing of wrought gold. He has God's loving-kindness, which is better than life. He can look on the hills and valleys and resplendent rivers, and say, 'My Father made them all.' 'All things are yours. Whether Paul, or Apollos, or Cephas, or the world, or life, or things present, or things to come; all are yours. Having nothing, yet possessing all things.'

February *twenty-sixth*

Cleansed

... and the blood of Jesus Christ his Son cleanseth us from all sin.
I John 1 v 7

There is nothing so defiling as our sins. Every one now redeemed was once all stained and defiled with sin - was once plunged in the miry clay. John Bunyan says, 'An unconverted man is the most doleful of all creatures.' One walking by the sea, said, 'My heart would pollute all that ocean.' Sin is an infinite evil. It leaves a mark on the soul that nothing human can wipe away. Oh! pray for a discovery of the loathsomeness of sin.

One thing is greater, the blood of Jesus, His own blood, the blood of the Lamb. As the waters were higher than the highest mountains, so the blood can cover the highest sins. Where sin abounded, grace did much more abound. It is atoning blood.

'There is a fountain fill'd with blood,
Drawn from Immanuel's veins;
And sinners plunged beneath that flood,
Lose all their guilty stains.'

Counterfeit conversion

The four and twenty elders fall down before him that sat on the throne, and worship him that liveth for ever and ever, and cast their crowns before the throne ...
Revelation 4 v 10

It is the clear mark of a hypocrite, that he is willing to cast his crown at the feet of a creature. Every jewel has its counterfeit, so there is a counterfeit conversion. Satan often changes people, and makes them think they are converted. These will give the glory to man. They cast their crown at the feet of a fellow worm and say, To him be glory. But one who is truly saved looks far above man, to Jesus, and says, 'To Him be glory.' A man healed by the brazen serpent would never attribute it to the pole, or the man that held it. He would look steadily to the blazing sign that God had set up. A man saved by Jesus will say to all eternity, To him be glory - 'Salvation to our God.' And when he comes into the New Jerusalem, he will not stop to look at the angels, nor fondly gaze on the redeemed, but will hasten to where Jesus sits, and fall down and worship and adore Him, casting his crown at His feet, and crying, 'Thou art worthy - Worthy is the Lamb that was slain.'

A silent sermon

For as often as ye eat this bread, and drink this cup, ye do shew the Lord's death till he come.
I Corinthians 11 v 26

Dear friends, it is this that is set before you in the broken bread and poured out wine - the whole work of Christ for the salvation of sinners. The love and grace of the Lord Jesus are all gathered into a focus there. The love of the Father; the covenant with the Son; the love of Jesus; His incarnation, obedience, death; all are set before you in that broken bread and wine. It is a sweet, silent sermon. Many a sermon contains not Christ from beginning to end. Many show Him doubtfully and imperfectly. But here is nothing else but Christ, and Him crucified. Most rich and speaking ordinance! Pray that the very sight of that broken bread may break your hearts, and make them flow to the Lamb of God. Pray for conversions from the sight of the broken bread and poured out wine. Look attentively, dear souls and little children, when the bread is broken and the wine poured out. It is a heart-affecting sight. May the Holy Spirit bless it. Dear believers, look you attentively, to get deeper, fuller views of the way of pardon and holiness. A look from the eye of Christ to Peter broke and melted his proud heart - he went out and wept bitterly. Pray that a single look of that broken bread may do the same for you. When the dying thief looked on the pale face of Immanuel, and saw the holy majesty that beamed from His dying eye, he cried, Lord remember me! This broken bread reveals the same thing. May the same grace be given you, and may you breathe the cry, Lord remember me.

O get ripening views of Christ, dear believers. The corn in harvest sometimes ripens more in one day than in weeks before. So some Christians gain more grace in one day than for months before. Pray that this may be a ripening harvest day in your souls.

February *twenty-ninth*

Not 'till then

... thou knowest not now; but thou shalt know hereafter.
John 13 v 7

When this passing world is done,
When has sunk yon radiant sun,
When I stand with Christ on high,
Looking o'er life's history,
Then, Lord, shall I fully know,
Not till then, how much I owe.

When I stand before the throne,
Dressed in beauty not my own,
When I see Thee as Thou art,
Love Thee with unsinning heart,
Then, Lord, shall I fully know,
Not till then, how much I owe.

Chosen, not for good in me,
Wakened up from wrath to flee,
Hidden in the Saviour's side,
By the Spirit sanctified,
Teach me, Lord, on earth to show
By my love how much I owe.

Oft I walk beneath a cloud,
Dark as midnight's gloomy shroud;
But, when fear is at it's height,
Jesus comes, and all is light;
Blessed Jesus, bid me show
Doubting saints how much I owe.

When the praise of heaven I hear,
Loud as thunders to the ear,
Loud as many waters' noise,
Sweet as harp's melodious voice,
Then, Lord, shall I fully know,
Not till then, how much I owe.

~ Robert Murray McCheyne 1813 - 43
(The original hymn has nine verses)

Robert Murray McCheyne around 24 years of age.

March

> "
>
> *It was to me a golden day when I first became acquainted with a young man so full of Christ.*
>
> "

REV. ALEXANDER MOODY STUART

March *first*

Positive sin

But if any provide not for his own, and specially for those of his own house, he hath denied the faith, and is worse than an infidel.
I Timothy 5 v 8

If you do not worship God in your family, you are living in positive sin; you may be quite sure you do not care for the souls of your family. If you neglected to spread a meal for your children to eat, would it not be said that you did not care for their bodies? And if you do not lead your children and servants to the green pastures of God's Word, and to seek the living water, how plain is it that you do not care for their souls! Do it regularly, morning and evening. It is more needful than your daily food - more needful than your work. How vain and silly all your excuses will appear, when you look back from hell! Do it fully. Some clip off the psalm, and some the reading of the Word; and so the worship of God is reduced to a mockery. Do it in a spiritual, lively manner. Go to it as to a well of salvation. There is, perhaps, no means of grace more blessed. Let all your family be present without fail. - let none be absent.

March *second*

Be ready

For I am now ready to be offered, and the time of my departure is at hand.
II Timothy 4 v 6

Dear believers, be ready to leave your room for the golden harp, at a minute's warning; be ready to leave your desk for the throne of Jesus - your pen for the palm of victory; be ready to leave the market below, for the street of the new Jerusalem, where the redeemed shall walk. If you were in a sinking ship, you would not cling hard to bags of money - you would sit loose to all, and be ready to swim. This world is like a sinking ship, and those who grasp at its possessions will sink with it. Oh! 'buy as though you possessed not'; for 'the time is short.'

Wonderful love

... Christ also loved the church and gave himself for it;
Ephesians 5 v 25

This is unparalleled love. Love is known by the sacrifice it will make. In a fit of love, Herod would have given away the half of his kingdom. If you will sacrifice nothing, you love not. Hereby we know that men love not Christ - they will sacrifice nothing for Him. They will not leave a lust - a game - a companion, for Christ. 'Greater love than this hath no man.' But Christ gave Himself. Consider what a self. If He had created ten thousand millions of worlds, and given them away, it had been great love -had He given a million of angels; but He gave the Lord of angels - the Creator of worlds. 'Lo, I come.' He gave the pearl of heaven. O what a self! - Jesus! - all loveliness!

Parts of prayer

Let my prayer be set forth before thee ...
Psalm 141 v 2

I ought not to omit any of the parts of prayer - confession, adoration, thanksgiving, petition, and intercession. There is a fearful tendency to omit confession, proceeding from low views of God and His law - slight views of my heart and the sins of my past life. This must be resisted. There is a constant tendency to omit adoration, when I forget to whom I am speaking - when I rush heedlessly into the presence of Jehovah, without remembering His awful name and character - when I have little eyesight for His glory, and little admiration of His wonders. 'Where are the wise?' I have the native tendency of the heart to omit giving thanks. And yet it is specially commanded, (Phillipians 4 v. 6). Often when the heart is selfish - dead to the salvation of others - I omit intercession. And yet it especially is the spirit of the Great Advocate, who has the name of Israel always on His heart.

Perhaps every prayer need not have all these; but surely a day should not pass without some space being devoted to each.

March *fifth*

A promise for the Saviour

I will hold thine hand, and will keep thee ...
Isaiah 42 v 6

The figure here seems taken from a father and his little child. When a little child has to go over some very rough road, or travel in the darkness, or to wade through some deep waters, he says to his father, 'I fear I shall be lost; I shall not be able to go through.' 'Nay, do not fear,' the father answers: 'I will hold thine hand; I will keep thee.' Such are the words of the Father to His dear Son. I would not have dared to have imagined them, if I had not found them in the Bible.

When God called His Son to the work, it could not but be a fearful work in His eyes. Christ knew well the infinite number of men's sins; for He is the searcher of hearts and trier of reins. He knew also the infinite weight of God's anger against these sins; He saw the dark clouds of infinite vengeance that were ready to burst over the head of sinners; He saw the infinite deluge of eternal wrath that was to drown for ever the guilty world. And, oh! how dreadful His Father's anger was in His eyes; for He had known nothing but His infinite love from all eternity. Oh! how could He bear to lie down under that wrath? How could He bear to exchange the smile of His Father's love for the dark frown of His Father's anger? How could He bear, for the sake of vile sinners, to exchange the caresses of that God who is love, for the piercings and bruisings of His almighty hand? Surely the very thought would be agony. God here comforts His Son under the view: Yon sea of wrath is deep, its waves are dreadful; but 'I will hold thine hand; I will keep thee.'

March *sixth*

Needless tears

And God shall wipe away all tears from their eyes; and there shall be no more death, neither sorrow, nor crying, neither shall there be any more pain: for the former things are passed way.
Revelation 21 v 4

This world is a vale of tears. There are always some mourning. No sooner is the tear dried up on one cheek that it trickles down another. Those that are in Christ should weep as though they wept not; 'for the time is short.' Do you weep over those that died in the Lord? It is right to weep: 'Jesus wept.' Yet weep as though you wept not; 'for the time is short.' They are not lost, but gone before. The sun, when it sets, is not lost; it is gone to shine in another hemisphere; and so have they gone to shine in a brighter world. It is self-love that makes you mourn for them; for they are happy. You would not mourn if they were with a distant friend on earth - why do you mourn that they are with the sinner's Friend? 'They shall hunger no more, neither thirst any more, neither shall the sun light upon them, nor any heat; for the Lamb which is in the midst of the throne shall feed them, and shall lead them unto fountains of living waters; and God shall wipe away all tears from their eyes.' 'The time is short;' and you will follow after. A few days, and you may be leaning together on the bosom of Jesus; you are nearer them to-day than you were yesterday.

March *seventh*

Everlasting Remembrance

... thou shalt not be forgotten of me.
Isaiah 44 v 21

The Lord cannot forget you. If you stood before God in your own righteousness, then I see how you might be separated from His love and care; for your frames vary, your goodness is like the morning cloud and the early dew. But you stand before Him in Christ: and Christ is the same yesterday, today, and forever.

You shall be held in everlasting remembrance.

The world may forget you; your friends may forget you: for this is a forgetting world. You may not have a tombstone over your grave; but God will not forget you. Christ will put your name beside that of His faithful martyr, Antipas.

In life, in death, in eternity, thou 'shalt not be forgotten of me.'

March *eighth*

Fullness divine

... he that hath mercy on them shall lead them, even by the springs
of water shall he guide them.
Isaiah 49 v10

Put your finger on the promise, and plead, 'When the poor and needy see water, and there is none, I the Lord will hear them' (Isaiah 41 v. 17). Tell Him you are poor and needy. Spread put your wants before Him. Take your emptiness to His fullness. There in an infinite supply with Him for every thing you need, at the very moment you need it.

March *ninth*

A serious situation

Nevertheless I have somewhat against thee,
because thou hast left thy first love
Revelation 2 v 4

There are times when, like Ephesus, many of God's children lose their first love, Iniquity abounds, and the love of many waxes cold. Believers lose their close and tender walking with God. They go out of the holiest, and pray at a distance with a curtain between. They lose their fervency, sweetness, and fullness in secret prayer. They do not pour out their hearts to God.

They have lost their clear discovery of Christ. They see him but dimly. They have lost the sight of His beauty - the savour of His good ointment - the hold of His garment. They seek Him, but find Him not. They cannot stir up the heart to lay hold on Christ.

The Spirit dwells scantily in their soul. The living water seems almost dried up within them. The soul is dry and barren. Corruptions are strong: grace is very weak.

Love to the brethren fades. United prayer is forsaken. The little assembly no more appears beautiful. Compassion for the unconverted is low and cold. Sin is unrebuked, though committed under their eye.

Christ is not confessed before men. Perhaps the soul falls into sin, and is afraid to return; it stays far off from God, and lodges in the wilderness.

Ah! this is the case, I fear, with many, It is a fearfully dangerous time. Nothing but a visit of the free Spirit to your soul can persuade you to return.

Crowned

Henceforth there is laid up for me a crown of righteousness, which the Lord, the righteous judge, shall give me at that day: and not to me only, but unto all them also that love his appearing.
II Timothy 4 v 8

How sweet it will be when Christ puts on the crown on a sinner's brow! The just God and Saviour! Angels will shout for joy when they see the righteous Jesus crowning the sinners for whom He died. He will finish our redemption. He was crowned with thorns; He has been an advocate crowned with glory and majesty; but another step - He is to put on the crown of righteousness. All heaven and earth and hell own Him faithful and true, and righteous in all His ways. Oh! how sweet to be crowned by Jesus.

Below His feet

It is good for me that I have been afflicted;
that I might learn thy statutes.
Psalm 119 v 71

There are many of the graces of God's people that can only grow in time of affliction. There is a plant in the garden which the gardener tramples below his feet to make it grow better. So it is with many of the graces of God's children - they grow better by being tried.

March *twelfth*

Light for eternity

But this man, after he had offered one sacrifice for sins for ever,
sat down on the right hand of God;
Hebrews 10 v 12

This is a great work of Christ as our High Priest. For this it was needful that He should become man and die. Had he remained God alone in the bosom of His Father, He might have pitied us, but He could not have died for us, nor took our sins away. We must have perished. Every priest in the Old Testament was a type of Jesus in this; every lamb that was slain typified Jesus offering up His own body a sacrifice for our sins.

Let your eye rest there if you would be happy. Those few hours on Calvary, when the great High Priest was offering up the amazing sacrifice, give light for eternity to the believing soul. This only will cheer you in dying. Not your graces, not your love to Christ, not anything in you, but only this - Christ hath died. He loved me and gave Himself for me. Christ hath appeared to put away sin by the sacrifice of Himself.

March *thirteenth*

Joy

Yet I will rejoice in the Lord, I will joy in the God of my salvation.
Habakkuk 3 v18

The purest joy in the world is joy in Christ Jesus. When the Spirit is poured down, His people get very near and clear views of the Lord Jesus. They eat His flesh and drink His blood. They come to a personal cleaving to the Lord. They taste that the Lord is gracious. His blood and righteousness appear infinitely perfect, full, and free to their soul. They sit under His shadow with great delight. They rest in the clefts of the rock. Their defence is the munitions of rocks. They lean on the Beloved. They find infinite strength in Him for the use of their soul - grace for grace - all they can need in any hour of trial and suffering to the very end.

They go by Him to the Father. "We joy in God through our Lord Jesus Christ." We find a portion there - a shield, and exceeding great reward. This gives joy unspeakable and full of glory.

No condemnation

*Who is he that condemneth? It is Christ that died, yea rather, that is
risen again,who is even at the right hand of God, who also maketh
intercession for us.*
Romans 8 v 34

Paul looks round all the judges of the world - all who are skilled in
law and equity; he looks upward to the holy angels, whose su
perhuman sight pierces deep and far into the righteous govern-
ment of God; he looks up to God, the judge of all, who must do right -
whose ways are equal and perfect righteousness - and he asked, 'Who
shall condemn? It is Christ that died.' Christ has paid the uttermost
farthing: so that every judge must cry out, 'There is therefore now no
condemnation.'

A triumphant deathbed

*I have fought a good fight, I have finished my course,
I have kept the faith:*
II Timothy 4 v 7

I think the dying thief could say: I believe, and enter with joy into
Paradise; but he could not say: 'I have kept the faith.' This makes
the difference between a peaceful and triumphant death-bed. Paul
'bought the truth, and sold it not.' That good thing committed to him
he kept, by the Holy Ghost given unto him. He held the beginning of
his confidence steadfast unto the end.

Learn that perseverance in the faith is needful to a triumphant death-
bed. It is Christ, and Christ alone, that is our peace in dying; yet
the hand that has longest held him has the firmest hold. It is not our
perseverance that is our righteousness before God, but the doing and
dying of the Lord Jesus; and yet without perseverance in the faith ye
cannot be saved. Alas! you that turn aside to folly, you are preparing
clouds for your dying bed. Can you say you have kept the faith, poor
backslider?

March *sixteenth*

Like the planets

... I have finished my course.
II Timothy 4 v 7

The moment a soul is brought to Christ, he has a course to run: And as John fulfilled his course, he said, 'Whom think ye that I am? I am not he. But, behold, there cometh one after me, whose shoes of his feet I am not worthy to loose' (Acts 13 v. 25). Paul says: 'But none of these things move me, neither count I my life dear unto myself, so that I might finish my course with joy, and the ministry, which I have received of the Lord Jesus, to testify the gospel of the grace of God' (Acts 20 v. 24). 'Wherefore seeing we also are compassed about with so great a cloud of witnesses, let us lay aside every weight, and the sin which doth so easily beset us, and let us run with patience the race that is set before us' (Hebrews 12 v. 1). Every one has a different course. Like the planets, all do not shine in the same part of the sky. So every believer has his course - a work to do. One has the course of a minister, another the course of a master, another that of a servant. Each of us has a work to do for Christ; let us do it diligently. 'My meat is to do the will of him that sent me.'

March *seventeenth*

Reaching forth

For I will pour water on him that is thirsty ...
Isaiah 44 v 3

Some persons are contented when they come to Christ. They sink back, as it were, into an easy chair, they ask no more, they wish no more. This must not be. If you are thirsty believers, you will seek salvation as much after conversion as before it. 'Forgetting those things which are behind, and reaching forth unto those things which are before, press toward the mark for the prize of the high calling of God in Christ Jesus.

Companions

*I am a companion of all them that fear thee, and of them
that keep thy precepts.*
Psalm 119 v 63

In choosing connections or friends, O choose with regard to this - will they help or hinder your prayers? Will they go with you, and help you on your journey? Or will they be a drag upon your wheels? In going into companies, in reading books, choose with regard to this - will they fill your sails for heaven? If not, go not near them. In yielding to your affections, especially if you find them hindering your journey, drop them instantly. Never mind the consequences.

'If thy right hand offend thee, cut it off, and cast it from thee. It is better to enter into life maimed, than having two hands to be cast into hell-fire.'

'Wherefore let us lay aside every weight, and the sin that doth so easily beset us, and let us run with patience the race that is set before us, looking unto Jesus.'

Devoting yourself

for thou art my servant ....
Isaiah 44 v 21

When a man consents that Christ shall be his Surety, he feels that he is not his own, but bought with a price. So David felt: 'Truly I am thy servant; I am thy servant, and the son of thine handmaid: thou hast loosed my bonds.' So Paul felt, when he lay gasping on the ground: 'Lord, what wilt thou have me to do?' Before conversion, the unconverted thinks that he is his own: may I not do what I will with mine own? He was the willing slave of the devil. But when he sees the price laid down for him, he feels that the Lord has redeemed him out of the house of bondage. Now he says: 'I am the Lord's.' Now he is more the servant of the Lord than ever he was of the devil. Oh! dear Christians, would that I could see more of this among you, a devoting of yourselves unto the Lord: 'For thou art my servant.'

March *twentieth*

The touch that heals

*And Jesus, moved with compassion, put forth his hand
and touched him ...*
Mark 1 v 41

When the woman had spent her all upon physicians, and was nothing better, but rather worse, she heard of Jesus. Ah! said she, if I may but 'touch the hem of his garment I shall be made whole'. Jesus said to her: 'Daughter, be of good comfort, thy faith hath made thee whole.' Come, them, incurable, to Christ. Leprosy was always regarded as incurable. Accordingly, the leper came to Jesus, and worshipping, said, 'Lord if thou wilt thou canst make me clean.' Jesus said, 'I will, be thou clean.' And immediately his leprosy was cleansed. Some of you feel that your heart is desperately wicked; well, kneel to the Lord Jesus, and say: 'Lord, if thou wilt, thou canst make me clean.' You are a leper - incurable; Jesus is able - He is also willing to make you clean.

March *twenty-first*

The Comforter abides forever

*Let your conversation be without covetousness; and be content
with such things as ye have: for he hath said, I will never
leave thee, nor forsake thee.*
Hebrews 13 v 5

You may take these words as those of the Spirit, and then they are like those words in fourteenth of John - 'I will pray the Father, and he shall give you another Comforter, that he may abide with you for ever' - to abide with you for ever. It is the same as these words - 'I will never leave thee, nor forsake thee.' When God the Holy Spirit comes to a soul, He will never leave it. Some may often be made to say 'I think the Spirit will go away from me. But observe, He says, 'I will never leave thee, nor forsake thee.' David cried out in the bitterness of his soul. 'Take not thy Holy Spirit away from me.' Here is the answer - 'I will never leave thee, nor forsake thee.' God will never forsake the temple in which He dwells. He forsook the tabernacle in the wilderness, and He forsook the temple at Jerusalem; but He will never forsake the living temple.

From the cross to the throne

And said, Behold, I see the heavens opened, and the Son of man standing in the right hand of God.
Acts 7 v 56

When believing souls seek for peace and joy in believing, they do very generally confine their view to Christ upon the earth. They remember Him as the good Shepherd seeking the lost sheep, they look to Him sitting by the well of Samaria, they remember Him saying to the sick of the palsy: 'Be of good cheer, thy sins are forgiven thee.' But they too seldom think of looking where Stephen looked - to where Jesus is now; at the right hand of God.

Now, my friends, remember, if you would be whole Christians, you must look to a whole Christ. You must lift your eye from the cross to the throne, and you will find Him the same Saviour in all, 'the same yesterday, and today, and for ever'. I have already observed, that wherever Christ is mentioned as being at the right hand of God, He is spoken of as seated there upon His throne; here, and here only, are we told that he is standing. In other places He is described as enjoying His glory, and entered into His rest; but here He is described as risen from His throne, and standing at the right Hand of God.

He rises to intercede: 'He is able to save to the uttermost all that come unto God by Him, seeing He ever liveth to make intercession for them.'

How often would a believer be a castaway, if it were not for the great Intercessor! How often faith fails! - 'flesh and heart faint and fail'; but see here, Christ never fails. On the death-bed, often the mind is taken off the Saviour, by pains of body and distress of mind; but, oh! happy soul that has truly accepted Christ. See here, He rises from His throne to pray for you, when you cannot pray for yourself. Look up to Him with the eye of faith, and cry: 'Lord Jesus, receive my spirit.'

March *twenty-third*
The utmost farthing

Who was delivered for our offences, and was raised again
for our justification.
Romans 4 v 25

If you saw a criminal put into prison, and the prison doors closed behind him, and if you never saw him come out again, then you might well believe that he was still lying in prison, and still enduring the just sentence of the law. But if you saw the prison doors fly open, and the prisoner going free; if you saw him walking at large in the streets, then you would know at once that he had satisfied the justice of his country, that he had suffered all that it was needful to suffer, that he had paid the utmost farthing. So with the Lord Jesus; he was counted a criminal - the crimes of guilty sinners against God were all laid at His door, and he was condemned on account of them. He was hurried away to the death of the cross, and the gloomy prison-house of His rocky sepulchre where the stone was rolled to the mouth of the grave. If you never saw Him come out, then you might well believe that He was still enduring the just sentence of the law. But, lo! 'he is risen - he is not here' - 'Christ is risen indeed'. God, who was His judge, hath raised Him from the dead, and set Him at His own right hand in the heavenly places; so that you may be quite sure He has satisfied the justice of God. He has suffered everything that it was needful for Him to suffer - He has paid the utmost farthing.

March *twenty-fourth*

The second look

Behold, he cometh with clouds; and every eye shall see him, and they
also which pierced him: and all kindreds of the earth shall wail
because of him. Even so, Amen.
Revelation 1 v 7

The first look to Christ makes the sinner mourn; the second look to Christ makes the sinner rejoice. When the soul looks first to Christ, he sees half the truth. He sees the wrath of God against sin, that God is holy and must avenge sin, that he can by no means clear the guilty. He sees that God's wrath is infinite, When he looks to Christ again, he sees the other half of the truth. The love of God to the lost, that God has provided a surety free to all. It is this that fills the soul with joy. Oh, it is strange, that the same object should break the heart and heal it! A look to Christ wounds, a look to Christ heals. Many, I fear, have only a half look at Christ, and this causes only grief. Many are slow of heart to believe all that is spoken concerning Jesus. They believe all except that he is free to them. They do not see this glorious truth: 'That a crucified Jesus is free to every sinner in the world,' that Christ's all is free to all.

March *twenty-fifth*

Soul sickness

I charge you, O daughters of Jerusalem, if ye find my beloved,
that ye tell him, that I am sick of love.
Song of Solomon 5 v 8

In the parable, the bride told the daughters of Jerusalem that she was sick of love. This was the message she bade them carry; and when they asked her about her beloved, she gave them a rich and glowing description of his perfect beauty ending by saying: 'He is altogether lovely.'

So it is with the believer in time of darkness: 'He is sick of love.' When Christ is present to the soul, there is no feeling of sickness. Christ is the health of the countenance. When I have him full in my faith as a complete surety, a calm tranquillity is spread over the whole inner man, the pulse of the soul has a calm and easy flow, the heart rests in a present Saviour with a healthy, placid affection. The soul is contented with him, at rest in him: 'Return unto thy rest, O my soul.' There is no feeling of sickness. It is health to he bones; it is the very health of the soul to look upon Him, and to love Him.

March *twenty-sixth*

At the heart's door

I sleep, but my heart waketh: it is the voice of my
beloved that knocketh ...
Song of Solomon 5 v 2

Even believers have got doors upon their hearts. You would think, perhaps, that when once Christ has found an entrance into a poor sinner's heart, He would never find difficulty in getting in any more. You would think that as Samson carried off the gates of Gaza, bar and all, so Christ would carry away all the gates and bars from believing hearts; but no, there is still a door on the heart, and Christ stands and knocks. He would fain be in. It is not His pleasure that we should sit lonely and desolate. He would fain come into us, and sup with us, and we with him.

March *twenty-seventh*

Not so the believer

I opened to my beloved; but my beloved had withdrawn himself, and was gone: my soul failed when he spake: I sought him, but I could not find him; I called him, but he gave me no answer.

Song of Solomon 5 v 6

In the parable we find that, when the bride found her husband was gone, she did not return to her rest.; Oh, no! Her soul failed for his word. She listens, she seeks, she calls. She receives no answer. She asks the watchmen, but they wound her, and take away her veil; still she is not broken off from seeking. She sets the daughters of Jerusalem to seek along with her.

So is it with the believer. When the slothful believer is really awakened to feel that Christ has withdrawn Himself, and is gone, he is slothful no longer. Believers remain at ease only so long as they flatter themselves that all is well; but if they are made sensible, by a fall into sin, or by a fresh discovery of the wickedness of their heart, that Christ is away from them, they cannot rest. The world can rest quite well, even while they know that they are not in Christ. Satan lulls them into fatal repose. Not so the believer - he cannot rest.

March *twenty-eighth*

Holy rapture

The Lord hath appeared of old unto me, saying, Yea, I have loved thee with an everlasting love: therefore with loving kindness have I drawn thee.

Jeremiah 31 v 3

Does it give you no joy to feel that God thought upon you in love before the foundation of the world? That when He was alone from all eternity He gave you to the Son to be redeemed?

'Before I formed thee in the belly, I knew thee; and before thou camest forth out of the womb, I sanctified thee. 'Does it give you no joy to think that the Son of God thought on you with love before the world was: 'My delights were with the children of men.' That He came into the world bearing your name upon His heart, that he prayed for you on the night of His agony: 'Neither pray I for these alone, but for all those that shall believe on me through their word'. Does it give you no joy that he thought upon you in His bloody sweat, that He thought of you upon the cross, and intended these sufferings to be in your stead? Oh, little children, how it would lift your hearts in holy rapture above the world, above its vexing cares, its petty quarrels, its polluting pleasures, if you would keep this holy joy within, taking up the very word of your Lord: 'Father, thou lovedst me before the foundation of the world'!

March *twenty-ninth*

Go to Jesus

As soon as she heard that, she arose quickly,
and came unto him.
John 11 v 29

It is evident that Mary was the more deeply affected of the two sisters. Martha was able to go about, but Mary sat still in the house. She felt the absence of Christ more than Martha. She believed his word more, and when that word seemed to fail, Mary's heart was nearly broken. Ah! it is a deep sorrow when natural and spiritual grief come together. Affliction is easily borne if we have the smile of Jehovah's countenance.

Why does the mourner rise, and hastily drying her tears, with eager step leave the cottage door? Her friends who sat around her she seems quite to forget. 'The Master is come. 'Such is the presence of the Lord Jesus to mourners still. The world's comforters are all physicians of no value. Miserable comforters are they all. They have no balm for a wounded spirit. 'The heart knoweth its own bitterness.' But when the Master comes and calls us, the soul revives. There is life in His call, His voice speaks peace. 'In my ye shall have peace.' Mourners should rise up quickly, and go to Jesus. The bereaved should spread their sorrows at the feet of Christ.

March *thirtieth*

His glory reflected

For, behold, the darkness shall cover the earth, and gross
darkness the people: but the Lord shall arise upon thee,
and his glory shall be seen upon thee.
Isaiah 60 v 2

It has long been discovered that colour is nothing in the object, but is all thrown upon it by the sun, and reflected back again. The beautiful colours with which this lovely world is adorned all proceed from the sun. His glory is seen upon the earth. It is all the gift of the sun that the grass is of that refreshing green, and the rivers are lines of waving blue. It is all the gift of the sun that the flowers are tinged with their thousand glories, that the petal of the rose has its delicate blush, and the lily, that neither toils nor spins, a brightness that is greater than Solomon's. Now, my dear souls, this is the way in which you may be justified. You are dark, and vile, and worthless in yourselves; but Christ's glory shall be seen on you.

If you only consent to take Christ for your surety, His divine righteousness is all imputed to you; His sufferings, His obedience are both yours.

March *thirty-first*

God's providence

For all things are for your sakes ...
II Corinthians 4 v 15

All things are for your sakes. For the sake of believers this world was created - the sun made to rule the day, and the moon to rule the night; every shining star was made for them. All are kept in being for your sakes. Winds rise and fall, waves roar and are still, seasons revolve, seed-time and harvest, day and night - all for your sakes. 'All things are yours.

All events are for your sakes. Kingdoms rise and fall to save God's people. Nations are His rod, His saw and axe to hew out a way for the chariot of the everlasting gospel; even as Hiram's hewers in Lebanon and the Gibeonite drawers of water were building up the temple of God.

The enemies of the church are only a rod in God's hand. He will do his purpose with them, then break the rod in two, and cast it away.

Specially all the providences of believing families are for your sakes. When Christ is dealing with a believing family, you say, 'That is no matter of mine. What have I to do with it?' Ah, truly if you are of the world, you have no part or lot in it! But if you are Christ's, it is for your sake, to the intent that ye may believe. The dealings of Christ with believing families are very instructive, His afflictions and His comforts, His way.

O learn to bear one another's burdens, to see more of Christ's hand among you, to the intent that ye may believe!

There's not a plant that grows below
But makes His glory known;
And thunders roll and tempests blow
By order from the throne.

St. Peter's Church, Dundee.

April

> "
>
> *Love to Christ was the great secret of*
> *all his devotion and consistency.*
>
> "
>
>
>
> REV. JAMES HAMILTON

April *first*

Lie in the dust

Therefore his sisters sent unto him, saying, Lord, behold,
he whom thou lovest is sick.
John 11 v 3

I f a worldly person had been sending to Christ, he would have sent a very different argument. He would have said: he who loves thee is sick. Here is one who has believed on Thy name. Here is one that has confessed Thee before the world, suffered reproach and scorn for Thy sake. Martha and Mary knew better how to plead with Jesus. The only argument was in Jesus' breast: 'He whom thou lovest is sick.'

Jesus loved him with an electing love: freely from all eternity Jesus loved him. Jesus loved him with a drawing love: He drew Him from under wrath, from serving sin. Jesus loved him with a pardoning love: He drew him to himself, and blotted out all his sin. Jesus loved him with an upholding love: 'Who could hold me up but thou?' He for whom Thou died, he whom Thou hast chosen, washed and kept till now, 'he whom thou lovest is sick'.

Learn thus to plead with Christ, dear believers. Often you do not receive, because you do not ask aright: 'ye ask, and receive not because ye ask amiss, that ye may consume it upon your lusts.' Often you ask proudly, as if you were somebody; so that if Christ were to grant it, He would only be fattening your lusts. Learn to lie in the dust, and plead only His own free love. Thou hast loved me for no good thing in me:

Chosen, not for good in me;
Wakened up from wrath to flee;
Hidden in the Saviour's side;
By the Spirit sanctified.

April *second*

Our continuing city

For he looked for a city which hath foundations,
whose builder and maker is God.
Hebrews 11 v 10

C hristians, learn to long for the heavenly Jerusalem. Do not forget it. Here we are in a strange land; be not taken up with any thing that is there. But yonder is our continuing city, the heavenly Jerusalem, with its pearly gates, and streets of shining gold. Let the chief of your desires be to be with Christ, which is far better. When the world is at the brightest, when friends are at the kindest, when your sky is at the clearest, still lift up this sweet song: 'If I forget thee, O Jerusalem, let my right hand forget her cunning. If I do not remember thee, let my tongue cleave to the roof of my mouth; if I prefer not Jerusalem above my chief joy.'

April *third*

Not ashamed

For I am not ashamed of the gospel of Christ: for it is the
power of God unto salvation to every one that believeth;
to the Jew first, and also to the Greek.
Romans 1 v 16

I am not ashamed of the gospel of Christ. More is meant in these words than is expressed. He does not mean only that he was not ashamed of the gospel, but that he gloried in it. It is very similar to Galatians 6 v. 14: 'But God forbid that I should glory, save in the cross of our Lord Jesus Christ.' Two things are implied in this.

Firstly, Paul was not ashamed of it before God. He had ventured his own soul on this way of Salvation. He could say, like David, 'This is all my salvation, this is all my desire.' The way of salvation by Jehovah our Righteousness was sweet to Paul. His soul rested there with great delight. He came thus to God in secret, thus in public, thus in dying. He hoped to stand before God through all eternity clothed in this divine righteousness. Secondly, he was not ashamed of it before men. Though all the world had been against him, Paul would have gloried in this way of salvation. He had a burning desire to make it known to other men. He felt it so sweet, he saw it to be so glorious, that he could have desired a voice so loud that all men might hear at one moment the way of salvation by Christ.

April *fourth*

Pride of grace

And lest I should be exalted above measure through the abundance
of the revelations, there was given to me a thorn in the flesh,
the messenger of Satan to buffet me, lest I should be exalted
above measure.
II Corinthians 12 v 7

Lest he should be exalted above measure. This is twice stated. What a singular thing is pride! Who would have thought that taking Paul into paradise for a day would have made him proud? And yet God, who new his heart, knew it would be so, and therefore brought him down to the dust.

The pride of nature is wonderful. A natural man is proud of anything. Proud of his person - although he did not make it, yet he prides himself upon his looks. Proud of his dress - although a block of wood might have the same cause for pride, if you would put the clothes on it. Proud of riches - as if there were some merit in having more gold than others. Proud of rank - as if there were some merit in having noble blood. Alas, pride flows in the veins. Yet, there is a pride more wonderful than that of nature - pride of grace. You would think a man never could be proud who had once seen himself lost. Yet, alas Scripture and experience show that a man may be proud of his measure of grace - proud of forgiveness, proud of humility, proud of knowing more of God than others. It was this that was springing up in Paul's heart when God sent him the thorn in the flesh.

April *fifth*

Precious to Him

The precious sons of Zion, comparable to fine gold, how are they esteemed as earthen pitchers, the work of the hands of the potter!
Lamentations 4 v 2

How amazing the love of Christ, that He died for us - such poor, weak flowers, and worms of a day! How safe are we in Jesus! Although we are nothing - fleeing like a shadow - yet in Him we abide for ever. Our very dust is precious dust to Him. Body and soul He will bring with Him, and we shall reign for ever and ever. O you that are in Christ, prize Him! You that are in doubt, solve it now by hasting to Him. You that are out of Him, choose Him now.

The first mark
... *for, behold, he prayeth*
Acts 9 v 11

Behold, he prayeth,' was the first mark that Paul was brought from death to life. The soul enjoys great nearness to God, enters within the veil, lies down at the feet of Jesus, and there pours out its groans and tears. The believer rises, like his Lord, a great while before day; or waking in the night, he cries in secret to God. Before entering any company, or by appointment meeting a friend, or answering a proposal, his heart wings its way to the mercy-seat. He prays without ceasing. He pours forth earnest cries for the deliverance from sin; the sins he is most tempted to, he prays most against. His intercessions for others are deep, constant, wide. It is sweet and easy for him to pray for others; 'Forbid that I should sin against God by ceasing to pray for you.'

God forsaken by God
... *My God, my God, why hast thou forsaken me?*
Matthew 27 v 46

These are the words of the great Surety of sinners, as He hung upon the accursed tree. The more I meditate upon them, the more impossible do I find it to unfold all that is contained in them. You must often have observed how a very small thing may be an index of something great going on within. The pennant at the mast-head is a small thing; yet it shows plainly which way the wind blows. A cloud no bigger than a man's hand is a small thing; yet it may show the approach of a mighty storm. The swallow is a little bird; and yet it shows that summer is come. So it is with man. A look, a sigh, a half-uttered word, a broken sentence may show more of what is passing within than a long speech. So it was with the dying Saviour. These few troubled words tell more than volumes of divinity.

A conversation in heaven

Thus saith God the Lord, He that created the heavens, and stretched
them out; he that spread forth the earth, and that which cometh out
of it; he that giveth breath unto the people upon it, and spirit to them
that walk therein: I the Lord have called thee in righteousness, and
will hold thine hand, and will keep thee, and give thee for a covenant
of the people, for a light of the Gentiles; To open the blind eyes, to
bring out the prisoners from the prison, and them that sit in darkness
out of the prison house. I am the Lord: that is my name: and my glory
will I not give to another, neither my praise to graven images.
Isaiah 42 vs 5 - 8

In this passage we have some of the most wonderful words that ever were uttered in the world. It is not a man speaking to a man. It is not even God speaking to a man. It is God speaking to His own Son. Oh, who would not listen? It is as if we were secretly admitted into the counsel of God, as if we stood behind the curtains of His dwelling-place, or were hidden in the clefts of the rock, and overheard the words of the eternal Father to the eternal Son.. Now sometimes when you overhear a conversation on earth, between two poor perishing worms, you think it is worth treasuring up; you remember what they said; you repeat it over and over again. Oh! then, when you overhear a conversation in heaven, when God the Father speaks, and God the Son stands to receive his words, will you not listen? Will you not lay up all these sayings in your heart?

God tells the Son: (1) That He had called Him to this service - had passed over all His angels, and chosen Him for this difficult work, (2) He tells Him that He is not to shrink from the difficulties of it. There is an ocean of wrath to wade through, but fear not; I will hold Thee by the hand - I will keep thee. (3) He tells Him that He must be given as a covenant Saviour. However dear to His heart, still, says God, 'I will give thee.' (4 He encourages Him by the great benefit to be gained - that he would be a light to whole nations of poor, blind, captive sinners. (5) That in all this He would have His glory: 'My glory will I not give to another, nor my praise to graven images.'

Something to hide

Thy word have I hid in mine heart, that I might not sin against thee.
Psalm 119 v 11

When Jesus makes holy, it is by writing the word in the heart: "Sanctify them through thy truth." When a mother nurses her child, she not only bears it in her arms, but holds it to her breast, and feeds it with the milk of her own breast; so does the Lord. He not only holds the soul, but feeds it with the milk of the Word. The words of the Bible are just the breathings of God's heart. He fills the heart with these, to make us like God. When you go much with a companion, and hear his words, you are gradually changed by them into his likeness; so when you go with Christ, and hear His words you are sanctified.

The deceitful heart

The heart is deceitful above all things, and desperately wicked: who can know it?
I the Lord search the heart, I try the reins, even to give every man according to his ways, and according to the fruit of his doings.
Jeremiah 17 v 9, 10

This is a faithful description of the natural heart of man. The heart of unfallen Adam was very different. 'God made man upright.' His mind was clear and heavenly. It was riveted upon divine things. He saw their glory without any cloud or dimness. His heart was right with God. His affections flowed sweetly and fully towards God. He loved as God loved, hated as God hated. There was no deceit about his heart then. It was transparent as crystal. He had nothing to conceal. There was no wickedness in his heart, no spring of hatred, or lust, or pride. He knew his own heart, He could see clearly into its deepest recesses; for it was just a reflection of the heart of God.

When Adam sinned, his heart was changed. When he lost the favour of God, he lost the image of God. Just as Nebuchadnezzar suddenly got a beast's heart, so Adam suddenly got a heart in the image of the devil. And this is the description ever since: 'The heart is deceitful above all things, and desperately wicked.'

April *eleventh*

Send up this cry

Wilt thou not revive us again: that thy people may rejoice in thee?
Psalm 85 v 6

The soul of a believer needs grace every moment. "By the grace of God I am what I am." But there are times when he needs more grace than at other times. Just as the body continually needs food; but there are times when it needs more food than at others - times of great bodily exertion, when all the powers are to be put forth.

Sometimes the soul of a believer is exposed to hot persecution. Reproach breaks the heart; or it beats like a scorching sun upon the head. "For my love they are my adversaries." Sometimes they are God's children who reproach us, and this is still harder to bear. The soul is ready to fret or sink under it.

Sometimes it is flattery that tempts the soul. The world speaks well of us, and we are tempted to pride and vanity. This is still worse to bear.

Sometimes Satan strives within us, by stirring up fearful corruptions, till there is a tempest within. Oh, is there a tempted soul that reads these words? Jesus prays for thee. Pray for thyself. You need more peace. Nothing but the oil of the Spirit will feed the fire of grace when Satan is casting water on it. Send up this cry, "Wilt thou not revive us again?"

April *twelfth*

Avoiding sin

Then shall the kingdom of heaven be likened unto ten virgins, which took their lamps, and went forth to meet the bridegroom.
Matthew 25 v 1

The truest mark of children of God is their avoiding sin. They flee from their old companions and old ways, they walk with God. And yet even this is imitated by the foolish virgins. They go out to meet their Lord. They flee old sins for a time, they hasten from their work to the house of God, they seek the company of God's children, perhaps they try to save others, and become very zealous in this. O how sad that many who now cling to the godly will soon be torn from them, and bound up with devils and wicked men!

It was good

When he had heard therefore that he was sick, he abode
two days still in the same place where he was.
John 11 v 6

Had Christ come at the first and healed their brother, we never would have known the love that showed itself at the grave of Lazarus, we never would have known the power of the great Redeemer in raising from the grave. These bright forth-shinings of the glory of Christ would have been lost to the Church and to the world. Therefore it was good that He stayed away for two days. Thus the honour of His name was spread far and wide. The Son of God was glorified. 'This people have I formed for myself; they shall show forth my praise.' This is God's great end in all His dealings with His people - that He may be seen. For this reason He destroyed the Egyptians: 'That the Egyptians may know that I am the Lord'

Why bread?

For I have received of the Lord that which also I delivered unto
you, That the Lord Jesus the same night in which he was
betrayed took bread: And when he had given thanks, he
brake it, and said, Take, eat: this is my body, which
is broken for you: this do in remembrance of me.
I Corinthians 11 vs 23-24

This day, my friends, I set before you the plainest and simplest picture of the silent sufferings of Jesus Christ, the Lamb of God. In that night in which He was betrayed, he took bread. Why bread? Firstly, because of its plainness and commonness. He did not take silver or gold or jewels, to represent His body, but bread, plain bread, to show you that when he came to be a surety for sinners, He did not come in His original glory, with His Father's angels. He took not on Him the nature of angels, he became man. Secondly, he chose bread to show you that He was dumb, and opened not His mouth. When I break the bread it resists not, it complains not, it yields to my hand. So it is with Christ. He resisted not, complained not, He yielded to the hand of infinite justice. 'He was led as a lamb to the slaughter, and as a sheep before her shearers is dumb, so he opened not his mouth.'

April *fifteenth*

An amazing weapon

For the preaching of the cross is to them that perish foolishness; but
unto us which are saved it is the power of God.
I Corinthians 1 v 18

To ungodly men nothing appears more weak and powerless than the gospel. They regard it as Lot's sons-in-law did his solemn warning: 'He seemed as one that mocked.' It appears an idle tale, an old wife's fable; but it is in reality 'the power of God unto salvation.' The gospel is an amazing weapon, when God wields it: 'The weapons of our warfare are not carnal, but mighty through God to the pulling down of strongholds.' When God wields the gospel, it is mighty to awaken the hardest hearts. Paul felt this in his own experience. He was a proud blasphemer, persecutor, and injurious - a proud, self-righteous Pharisee. You would have said: 'Nothing in the world can awaken that man.' Jesus revealed Himself to him, and he fell to the ground, trembling and astonished. So he had seen it in the case of others: in Lydia and the jailer, in Sergius Paulus, the deputy of Cyprus: 'He believed, being astonished at the doctrine of the Lord' (Acts 13 v. 12). 'The power of God unto salvation!' Not God's mighty arm to destroy, but His mighty arm to save.

April *sixteenth*

A good thing

And the ark of the Lord continued in the house of Obed-edom
the Gittite three months: and the Lord blessed Obed-edom,
and all his household.
II Samuel 6 v 11

When the ark of God was carried into the house of Obed-edom the Gittite, and remained there three months, then it is said the Lord blessed Obed-edom, and his household, and all that he had. Now, every believer is a kind of ark of God in which he hides His law, every believer is a temple of the Holy Ghost. It is a good thing to receive a believer unto our house, for the blessing of God goes with him. That promise is true to him: 'Blessed is he that blesseth thee, cursed is he that curseth thee.'

As far back as the flood you remember how wicked Ham was saved in the ark, and kept from being devoured with the wicked world, because he was in righteous Noah's family. Doubtless many an ungodly son among us is kept alive, and spared a little longer because of his righteous father.

You remember how Sodom would have been spared if there had been ten righteous men found in it; and how the angel told Lot, 'I cannot do any thing until thou be escaped thither.' Doubtless, this town in which we live is spared only for the sake of the few children of God that are in it. Take them away, and God's wrath would doubtless come down immediately. How little you think, my unconverted friends, that you owe it to the children of God, whom you despise, that you are not this day in hell.

Misers of grace

And of his fulness have all we received, and grace for grace.
John 1 v 16

A Christian in our day is like a man who has got a great reservoir brimful of water. He is at liberty to drink as much as he pleases, for he never can drink it dry; but instead of drinking the full stream that flows from it, he dams it up, and is content to drink the few drops that trickle through. O that ye would draw out of His fullness, ye that have come to Christ! Do not be misers of grace. There is far more than you will use in eternity. The same waters are now in Christ that refreshed Paul, that gave Peter his boldness, that gave John his affectionate tenderness. Why is your soul less richly supplied than theirs? Because you will not drink: 'If any man thirst, let him come unto me, and drink.'

April *eighteenth*

Heavenly tenderness

Nevertheless I tell you the truth; It is expedient for you that I go away: for if I go not away, the Comforter will not come unto you; but if I depart, I will send him unto you.
John 16 v 7

When friends are about to part from one another, they are far kinder than ever they have been before. It was so with Jesus. He was going to part from His disciples, and never till now did His heart flow out toward them in so many streams of heavenly tenderness. Sorrow had filled their heart, and therefore divinest compassion filled His heart. 'I tell you the truth, it is expedient for you that I go away.'

Surely it was expedient for Himself that He should go away. He had lived a life of weariness and painfulness, not having where to lay His head, and surely it was pleasant in His eyes that He was about to enter into His rest. He had lived in obscurity and poverty - He gave His back to the smiters, and His cheeks to them that plucked off the hair. Now, surely, He might well look forward with joy to His return to that glory which He had with the Father before ever the world was, when all the angels of God worshipped Him. And yet He does not say: 'It is expedient for me that I go away.' Surely that would have been comfort enough to His disciples. But no: he says: 'It is expedient for you.' He forgets Himself altogether, and thinks only of His little flock which He was leaving behind Him: 'It is expedient for you that I go away.' O most generous of Saviours! He looked not on His own things, but on the things of others also. He knew that it is far more blessed to give than it is to receive.

April *ninteenth*

Looking at Christ

But made himself of no reputation, and took upon him the form of a servant, and was made in the likeness of men:
Philippians 2 v 7

He was the eternal Son of God - equal with the Father in every thing, therefore equal in happiness. He had glory with Him before ever the world was. Yet His happiness also consisted in giving. He was far above all the angels, and therefore He gave far more than they all: 'The Son of Man came not to be ministered unto, but to minister, and to give His life a ransom for many.' He was highest, therefore He stooped lowest. They gave their willing services, He gave Himself: 'Ye know the grace of our Lord Jesus Christ, that though he was rich, yet for our sakes he became poor, that we, through his poverty, might be made rich, Let this mind be in you which was also in Christ.'

Now, dear Christians, some of you pray night and day to be branches of the true Vine; you pray to be made all over in the image of Christ. If so, you must be like Him in giving. A branch bears the same kind of fruit as the tree. If you be branches at all, you must bear the same fruit. An old divine says well: 'What would have become of us if Christ had been as saving of His blood as some men are of their money?'

April twentieth

Only one sin

For as by one man's disobedience many were made sinners, so by the obedience of one shall many be made righteous.
Romans 5 v 19

Only one sin. Some of you see little evil in one sin, or in a hundred sins; but here you see one sin cast Adam and all his children out of paradise. God did not wait till it was repeated. It appeared a small sin. The outward action was small - only stretching out the hand and taking an inviting fruit. Some of you think little of sins that make no great noise; such as breaking the Sabbath, drinking too much, speaking what is false, sitting down Christless at the Lord's table; but see here, one small sin brought a world under the curse of God. God would rather a world should perish than one small sin go unpunished.

April twenty-first

Remember the sabbath day

I was in the Spirit on the Lord's day ...
Revelation 1 v 10

John was keeping the Christian Sabbath in Patmos. Even though an exile, far from fellow-christians, he was walking in the Spirit when God gave this blessed vision to him. Thus, my friends, even when away from the house of God, if you will seek to be in the Spirit, and to honour the Sabbath, God will make up for the want of ordinances.

April *twenty-second*

The comforter

Now I beseech you, brethren, for the Lord Jesus Christ's sake,
and for the love of the Spirit, that ye strive together
with me in your prayers to God for me.
Romans 15 v 30

It is curious to remark, that wherever the Holy Ghost is spoken of in the Bible, He is spoken of in terns of gentleness and love. We often read of the wrath of God the Father, as in Romans 1 v 18 'The wrath of God is revealed from heaven against all ungodliness and unrighteousness of men.' And we often read of the wrath of God the Son : 'Kiss the Son, lest he be angry, and ye perish from the way'; or, 'Revealed from heaven taking vengeance.' But we nowhere read of the wrath of God the Holy Ghost.

He is compared to a dove, the gentlest of all creatures. He is warm and gentle as the breath: 'Jesus breathed on them, and said, Receive ye the Holy Ghost.' He is gentle as the falling dew: 'I will be as the dew unto Israel.' He is soft and gentle as oil; for He is called, 'The oil of gladness.' The fine oil wherewith the high priest was anointed was a type of the Spirit. He is gentle and refreshing as the springing well: 'The water that I shall give him shall be in him a well of water springing up unto everlasting life.' He is called 'The Spirit of grace and of supplications.'

He is nowhere called the Spirit of wrath. He is called the 'Holy Ghost, which is the Comforter.' Nowhere is he called the Avenger. We are told that He groans within the heart of a believer, 'helping his infirmities'; so that He greatly helps the believer in prayer. We are told also of the love of the Spirit - nowhere of the wrath of the Spirit. We are told of His being grieved: 'Grieve not the Holy Spirit'; of His being resisted: 'Ye do always resist the Holy Ghost'; of His being quenched: 'Quench not the Spirit.' But these are all marks of gentleness and love.

Nowhere will you find one mark of anger or of vengeance attributed to Him; and yet, brethren, when this blessed Spirit begins His work of love, mark how He begins - He convinces of sin. Even He, all-wise, almighty, all-gentle and loving though he be, cannot persuade a poor sinful heart to embrace the Saviour, withour first opening up His wounds and convincing him that he is lost.

Equally righteous

*I will greatly rejoice in the Lord, my soul shall be joyful in
my God; for he hath clothed me with the garments of
salvation, he hath covered me with the robe of
righteousness, as a bridegroom decketh himself with
ornaments, and as a bride adorneth
herself with her jewels.*
Isaiah 61 v 10

I have seen a family of children all dressed alike, that none might boast over the others, all being equally fair. So it is with God's family. They are all righteous in the obedience of one. One garment covers them all - the robe of their elder Brother. Believers differ in attainments, in gifts and graces, but all are equally justified before God. It is not work of their own that justifies them, it is the work of Christ alone. Ah, brethren! there in so boasting in Christ's family.

None but Jesus

*Into thine hand I commit my spirit: thou hast redeemed
me, O Lord God of truth.*
Psalm 31 v 5

Some Christians have little affliction. They sail on a smooth sea, they enjoy health of body for years together, they never knew what it was to want a comfortable meal. Death has perhaps not once entered their dwelling. They think it will be always thus. But a change comes. The 'harp of thousand strings' becomes our tune. The 'clay cottage' gives tokens of decay, or grim want invades their dwelling, or death comes up into the window. Ah! it is hard to bear. 'No affliction for the present seems to be joyous, but grievous.' Who can comfort? None but Jesus. He knew all sorrow, deeper sorrows than we have ever known, or will ever know. His heart is not of stone. He feels along with us. He afflicts not willingly. He seeks to bring us more to himself. O afflicted believer, commit thy weeping, suffering, pining, trembling soul to Jesus: 'Into thine hand I commit my spirit.'

April *twenty-fifth*

The righteousness of God

For therein is the righteousness of God revealed from faith to faith:
as it is written, The just shall live by faith.
Romans 1 v 17

There is something infinitely vast and glorious in the righteousness of God. When the deluge covered the earth, it covered the highest mountains. Looking down from above, not one mountain-top could be seen, but a vast world of waters - a vast plain reflecting the beams of the sun. So if you this day lie down under the righteousness of God, the mountains of your sins will not be seen, but only the vast, deep, glorious righteousness of your God and Saviour. If you were to cast a stone into the deepest part of the ocean, it would be lost and swallowed up by the deep waves of ocean; so when a sinner is cast down under the righteousness of God, he is as it were lost and swallowed up in Christ.

April *twenty-sixth*

Fear not

By faith he forsook Egypt, not fearing the wrath of the king: for he
endured, as seeing him who is invisible.
Hebrews 11 v 27

You remember when Elisha and his servant were in Dothan, and a great host of enemies compassed them in, the young man cried, Alas, my master, how shall we do? and Elisha answered, Fear not, for they that be with us, are more than they that be with them. And Elisha prayed, and said, 'Lord, I pray thee, open his eyes that he may see.' And the Lord opened the eyes of the young man, and he saw, and behold, the mountain was full of horses and chariots of fire round about Elisha.

Dear brethren, believe what you do not see. Live by faith in a Covenant-keeping God. 'God is faithful, who also will do it.'

April *twenty-seventh*

Mark the change

And I will make of thee a great nation, and I will bless thee, and
make thy name great; and thou shalt be a blessing:
Genesis 12 v 2

Abraham, before his conversion, was doubtless as selfish and ungodly as any unconverted man among us. Doubtless he thought it beneath him to have family prayer, or to teach his children and servants to know the Saviour. Doubtless he was as cold and selfish in these things as most are among ourselves. But mark the change! When Abraham becomes a child of God, he builds a family altar wherever he goes; and though he had hundreds of servants under him, yet he cared anxiously for the souls of them all. 'For I know him,' says God, 'that he will command his servants and his household after him, to keep the ways of the Lord.' Before, he had been a curse; but now he is a blessing.

Dorcas before her conversion was doubtless as selfish, and as fond of worldly things, as all unconverted people are. Doubtless she thought it beneath her to make coats and garments for the poor, doubtless she was as selfish in these things as most are amongst us. But mark the change! When she becomes a child of God, then to do good and to distribute seems to have been the pleasure of her life. This woman was full of good works and alms-deeds, which she did. Before she had been a curse; but now she is a blessing.

Paul before his conversion was as great an enemy to the truth and as keen a persecutor of Christians as most unconverted persons are: 'I thought I should do many things contrary to the name of Jesus of Nazareth; I was a blasphemer, and persecutor, and injurious.' But mark the change, when he became a child of God: 'In the bowels of Jesus Christ I long after you all;' 'I will very gladly spend and be spent for you.'

Are you converted? Then see that you be a blessing. Once you were a curse. See that you be as much a blessing.

April *twenty-eighth*

Angels unawares

Be not forgetful to entertain strangers: for thereby some have entertained angels unawares.
Hebrews 13 v 2

You remember how a poor widow of Sarepta received Elijah into her house, and how he was a blessing to her; for her barrel of meal never wasted, and her cruse of oil never failed; and her son was brought to life again through Elijah's prayer. Ah, brethren, be careful to entertain the children of God, you will find them angels in disguise. Wherever a child of God is, God's eye is upon that spot by night and day. Oh, it is good to be near to the children of God, that we may share in their blessing. He that receiveth them receiveth Jesus. Blessed is he that blesseth them and cursed is he that curseth them.

April *twenty-ninth*

The Saviour's silence

He was oppressed and he was afflicted, yet he opened not his mouth:
Isaiah 53 v 7

Before the world was, He entered into covenant with His Father, that He would stand as a substitute for sinners; and therefore when He did come to suffer, His very righteousness sustained Him, and He set His face like a flint. When a feeble man undertakes some hard piece of service, very often he is loud and boastful before he begins; but when he comes up to the point, his courage dies, and he goes away back from his word. Not so the Son of God. He had sworn that he would bear the curse that was hanging over sinners. He had struck hands with the eternal Father He would be their Jonah, to lie down under their sea of wrath: 'Take me up,' he said, 'and cast me into that sea of wrath.' And so, when the waves and billows went over Him, he did not cry nor murmur. He set His face steadfastly. He had sworn once by His holiness, and He would not turn from it. He would not alter the thing that had gone out of His lips. 'He was led as a lamb to the slaughter, and as a sheep before her shearers is dumb, so he opened not his mouth.'

April *thirtieth*

Arise, shine!

Arise, shine; for thy light is come, and the glory
of the Lord is risen upon thee.
Isaiah 60 v 1

Christians are to become like Christ - little suns, to rise and shine upon a dark world. He rises and shines upon us, and then says to us, 'Arise, shine.' This is Christ's command to all on whom He has arisen. Dear Christians, 'ye are the light of the world.' Poor, and feeble, and dark, and sinful though ye be, Christ has arisen upon you for this very end, that you might arise and shine. Be like the sun, which shineth every day, and on every place. Wherever he goes he carries light; so do you. Some shine in public before men, but are dark as night in their own family. Dear Christian, look more to Christ, and you will shine more constantly. Make it the business of your life to shine. If the sun were to grow weary of running his daily journey, would you not say it should be taken down? Just so, if you grow weary in well-doing, in shining with Christ's beauty, you too should be taken down and cast away.

May

> "
>
> *I was often reproved by his unabated attention to personal holiness.*
>
> "
>
> ANDREW BONAR

May *first*

Partakers of one grace

He that reapeth receiveth wages, and gathereth fruit unto life eternal:
that both he that soweth and he that reapeth may rejoice together.
John 4 v 36

He that soweth and he that reapeth may rejoice together. Christian friends are sweet to the Christian. Those who are sharers of our spiritual secrets, those who mingle prayer with us before the throne, those who never forget us when within the veil - oh, there is something cheering in the very light of their kindly eye! It is an intercourse of which the world knows nothing. We have them in our heart, inasmuch as they are partakers of one grace, washed in one fountain, filled with the same Spirit, members one of another.

May *second*

Satan keeps me from it

But when the comforter is come, whom I will send unto you from
the Father, even the Spirit of truth, which proceedeth from the
Father, he shall testify of me:
John 15 v 26

I ought to study the Comforter more - His Godhead, His love, His almightiness. I have found by experience that nothing sanctifies me so much as meditating on the Comforter, as John 14 v. 16 'And I will pray the Father, and he shall give me another Comforter, that he may abide with you for ever;' And yet how seldom I do this! Satan keeps me from it. I am often like those men who said, They knew not if there be any Holy Ghost....I ought never to forget that my body is dwelt in by the Third Person of the Godhead. The very thought of this should make me tremble to sin, I Corinthians 6 V. 19 .....I ought never forget that sin grieves the Holy Spirit - vexes and quenches him.....If I would be filled with the Spirit, I feel I must read the Bible more, pray more, and watch more.

A Great Love

Behold what manner of love the Father hath bestowed upon us, that
we should be called the sons of God:
I John 3 v 1

How often in the day is the love of Christ quite out of view! How often is it obscured to us! How often are we left without a realising sense of the completeness of His offering. Is there any one of you desirous of being made new, of being delivered from the slavery of sinful habits and affections? We can point you to no other remedy but the love of Christ. Behold how He loved you! See what He bore for you; under a sense of your sin, flee to the Saviour of sinners. As the timorous dove flies to hide itself in the crevices of the rock, so do you flee to hide yourself in the wounds of your Saviour.

Use it right

And behold, I come quickly; and my reward is with me, to give
every man according as his work shall be.
Revelation 22 v 12

The whole Bible shows that Christians will be rewarded in eternity just in proportion to the use they have made of their talents. Now, money is one talent. If you use it right you will in no wise lose your reward. Christ plainly shows that He will reckon with men in the judgement according as they have dealt by His poor Christians. They that have done much for Christ shall have an abundant entrance; they that have done little shall have little reward

I thank God that there are some among you to whom Christ will say: 'Come, ye blessed of my Father, inherit the kingdom prepared for you from the foundation of the world.' Go on, dear Christians - live still for Christ. Never forget, day nor night, that you are yourselves bought with a price. Lay yourselves and your property all in His hand, and say: 'What wilt thou have me to do? Here am I, send me'; and then I know you will feel, now and in eternity. 'It is more blessed to give than to receive.'

May *fifth*

The heart of Christ

But we see Jesus, who was made a little lower than the angels for the
suffering of death, crowned with glory and honour; that he by the
grace of God should taste death for every man.
Hebrews 2 v 9

The four Gospels are a narrative of the heart of Christ. They show
His compassion to sinners, and His glorious work in their stead.
If you only knew that heart as it is, you would lay your weary
head with John on His bosom. Do not take up your time so much with
studying your own heart as with studying Christ's heart. 'For one look
at yourself, take ten looks at Christ!'

May *sixth*

Heaven's greatest wonder

Therefore doth my Father love me, because I lay down my life, that I
might take it again. No man taketh it from me, but I lay it down of
myself. I have power to lay it down, and I have power to take it
again. This commandment have I received of my Father.
John 10 vs 17 - 18

The death of Christ is, my friends, the most wonderful event past,
present, or future in the whole universe. It is so in the eye of God
- 'Therefore doth my Father love me, because I lay down my life.'
There is nothing in the whole world so lovely as His Son. It is not only
for His Godhead, but on account of his manhood, through which He
laid down His life - 'Therefore doth my Father love me, because I laid
down my life.' These words of Christ, 'I lay down my life,' are dearer to
God than a thousand worlds.

May *seventh*

Hell's greatest wonder

And having spoiled principalities and powers, he made a shew of
them openly, triumphing over them in it.
Colossians 2 v 15

The death of Christ is the greatest wonder in hell. This was one
thing which Satan did not know the meaning of - the death of
Christ. Ah! Satan thought when he got Judas to betray Him, and

the Jews to crucify Him, that he had prevailed against Him - that he had gained the victory; but ah! Satan hath found it out now, that Christ has triumphed over him in His cross. Ah! then, brethren, Calvary is a wonder in hell. Tell me then, brethren, who is it in all the universe that thinks little of Christ's laying down His life. Shall we find them in heaven? No. Shall we find them in Hell? No; 'they believe and tremble.' Where, then, shall we find the man that thinks little of Christ? O Christless sinner! it is you. 'We preach Christ, to the Jews a stumbling block, and to the Greeks foolishness.' 'For the preaching of the cross is, to them that perish, foolishness.' O Christless man! you little think of the death of Christ; even the devils do not think it foolishness. Sinner, do not you think there must be something wrong about the state of your mind, that sees no beauty in the death of Christ?

May *eighth*

Preparation

But seek ye first the kingdom of God, and his righteousness; and all these things shall be added unto you.
Matthew 6 v 33

A re you fitter for heaven every day? Ah! my dear Christians, I tremble for some of you who are on your way to glory. Oh! that you would forget the things that are behind, and reaching forth to those that are before, press forward toward the mark for the prize of the high calling of God in Christ Jesus. Some of you are just beginning the journey to Heaven. Pray more, read more, hear more, love more, do more every day.

May *ninth*

Live near to Christ

They shall perish; but thou remainest; and they all shall wax old as doth a garment.
Hebrews 1 v 11

R utherford says: 'Build your nest upon no tree here; for you see God hath sold the forest to Death, and every tree whereon we would rest is ready to be cut down, to the end we may flee and mount up, and build upon the Rock, and dwell in the holes of the Rock.'

Set not your heart on the flowers of this world; for they have all a canker in them. Prize the Rose of Sharon and the Lily of the Valley more than all; for He changeth not. Live nearer to Christ than to the saints, so that when they are taken from you, you may have Him to lean on still.

May *tenth*

Complete

And ye are complete in him, which is the head of all
principality and power:
Colossians 2 v 10

Learn how complete a Saviour Christ is. God did not choose a man to this great work. He did not choose an angel. He passed by them all, and chose His Son. Why? Because He saw none other could be a sufficient Saviour. If Christ had not been enough, God never would have called Him to it.. God knew well the weight of His own wrath; and, therefore, He provided an almighty back to bear it. Trembling sinner, do not doubt the completeness of Christ. God knew all your sins and your wrath when He chose Christ - that they were both infinite; and therefore He chose an almighty, an infinite Saviour. Oh! hide in Him, and you are complete in Him.

May *eleventh*

Likeness to Jesus

Then said he unto Zebah and Zalmunna, What manner of men were
they whom ye slew at Tabor? And they answered, As thou art, so
were they; each one resembled the children of a king.
Judges 8 v 18

It is not so much great talents that God blesses, as a great likeness to Jesus.

The true value of an action

Talk no more so exceeding proudly; let not arrogancy come out
of your mouth: for the Lord is a God of knowledge,
and by him actions are weighed.
I Samuel 2 v 3

In order to know the true value of an action, you must search the heart. Many a deed that is applauded by men, is abominable in the sight of God, who searches the heart. To give an alms to a poor man may be an action either worthy of an eternal reward, or worthy of an eternal punishment. If it be done out of love to Christ, because the poor man is a disciple of Christ, it will in no wise lose its reward. Christ will say: 'Inasmuch as ye did it to the least of these my brethren, ye did it unto me.' If it be done out of pride or self-righteousness, Christ will cast it from Him; He will say, 'Depart, ye cursed; ye did it not unto me.'

Higher upon the rock

From the end of the earth will I cry unto thee, when my heart is
overwhelmed: lead me to the rock that is higher than I.
Psalm 61 v 2

Every wave of trouble for Christ's sake lifts the soul higher upon the Rock. Every arrow of bitterness shot after the believer makes him hide farther back in the clefts of Jesus. Be content dear friend, to bear these troubles which make you cling closer to your Beloved.

Pure joy

Charge them that are rich in this world, that they be not highminded,
nor trust in uncertain riches, but in the living God,
who giveth us richly all things to enjoy;
I Timothy 6 v 17

It is quite right for a believer to use the things of this world, and to rejoice in them. None has such a right as the believer has to rejoice and be happy. He has a right to use the bodily comforts of this world - to eat his meat 'with gladness and singleness of heart, praising God'. He has a right to all the joys of home, and kindred, and friendship. It is highly proper that he should enjoy these things. He has a right to all the pure pleasures of mind, of intellect, and imagination; for God has given him all things richly to enjoy.

Still, he should 'rejoice as though he rejoiced not, and use this world as not abusing it'; for 'the time is short'. In a little while, you will be at your Father's table above, drinking the new wine with Christ. You will meet with all your brothers and sisters in Christ - you will have pure joy in God through ceaseless ages.

May *fifteenth*

Wide open

And as Moses lifted up the serpent in the wilderness,
even so must the Son of man be lifted up:
John 3 v 14

The whole Bible shows that Christ is quite willing and anxious that all sinners should come to Him. The city of refuge in the Old Testament was a type of Christ; and you remember that its gates were open by night and by day. The arms of Christ were nailed wide open, when He hung upon the cross; and this was a figure of His wide willingness to save all, as He said: 'I, if I be lifted up from the earth, will draw all men unto me.' But though His arms were firmly nailed, they are more firmly nailed wide open now, by His love and compassion for perishing sinners, than ever they were nailed to the tree.

May *sixteenth*

Eternity

It is a fearful thing to fall into the hands of the living God.
Hebrews 10 v 31

In the time of health and strength, it is common for men to boast against God. They are not in trouble as other men, neither are they plagued like other men; therefore pride compasseth them about as a chain. They can sin with a high hand. But when they are brought to the brink of the grave by fever or wasting consumption - when they need someone to turn them on their bed, or to hold up their fainting head, or to feed them like a child - then we see that a sinner is nothing in the hands of an angry God.

And O what will it be in eternity, when he falls into the hands of the living God! Perhaps he doubted whether there was a God; but all of a sudden he sees there is a God. He thought there was no hell, and laughed at those who believed it - in a moment he is tossing among its fiery waves; and now he feels it must be eternal. After a thousand years it is but beginning, and no nearer an end. The soul will sink into insupportable gloom - it will wish to die, and not be able. 'What if God, willing to show His wrath, and to make His power known, endured with much long-suffering the vessels of wrath, fitted to destruction?' O brethren, flee from the wrath to come! You cannot bear it. Can you bear a fever or the stroke of palsy, or a strike of lightning, or wasting consumption? And these are but the little finger of the hand of God's anger.

May *seventeenth*

Sweet and easy

Many therefore of his disciples, when they had heard this, said, This is an hard saying; who can hear it?
John 6 v 60

A great many persons are much taken with Christ; they have some anxiety about their souls; they follow anxiously after the preaching of the Word; but when we show them that Christ is the bread of heaven, that they must have a personal closing with Christ, as much as if they were to eat His flesh and drink His blood, these souls say; 'It is a hard saying, who can bear it?' By-and-by, they are offended, they believe not, they go back and walk no more with Jesus. Is any hearing me in this condition? Oh! think again, I beseech you, before you go back. Oh! seek the teaching of God, and He will show you that none of Christ's sayings are hard sayings, but that they are all sweet and easy. When the heart of a poor Indian was brought under the teaching of God, he said: 'Some people complain that the Bible is a hard book; but I have not read so far as to find it a hard book. To me it is all sweet and easy.'

May *eighteenth*

Christk our righteous

For as in Adam all die, even so in Christ shall all be made alive.
I Corinthians 15 v 22

We have seen that in the fall and ruin of man, it pleased God to deal with man, not as a field of corn, each standing on his own root, but as a tree, in which all the branches stand or fall together. We were not made sinners, each by his individual sin, but all by the sin of one. In like manner it has pleased God to justify sinners, not each by his own obedience, by his own goodness and holiness, but 'by the obedience of one.' Just as Adam by his one sin brought death, the curse of God, and total spiritual death, not only upon himself, but upon all his branches, even the most distant, even the minutest, even though unborn; so the second Adam, by His own obedience, brought pardon, righteousness, spiritual life, and eternal glory to all His branches, even the most distant, the smallest, even those unborn.

May *ninteenth*

Learn to stoop low

Him that is weak in the faith receive ye,
but not to doubtful disputations.
Romans 14 v 1
We then that are strong ought to bear the infirmities of the weak,
and not to please ourselves.
Romans 15 v 1

There is much of an opposite spirit, I fear, amongst us. I fear that you love our Marys and Pauls and Johns, you highly esteem those that are evidently pillars. But can you condescend to men of low estate? Learn to stoop low, and to be gentle and kind to the feeble. Do not speak evil of them, do not make their blemishes the subject of your common talk. Cover their faults. Assist them by counsel, and pray for them.

A Golden saying

*And I heard a voice from heaven saying unto me, Write, Blessed
are the dead which die in the Lord from henceforth: Yea, saith
the Spirit, that they may rest from their labours; and their
works do follow them.*
Revelation 14 v 13

Blessed are the dead. Learn the value of this saying. It is a golden saying - there is gold in every syllable of it. It is sweeter than honey and the honeycomb, more precious than gold, yea, much fine gold. It is precious in the eyes of God. Write it deep in your hearts; it will solemnise your life, and will keep you from being led away by its vain show. It will make the syren songs of this world inconvenient and out of tune; it will sweetly soothe you in the hour of adversity; it will rob death of its sting, and the grave of its victory. Write, write deep on your heart, 'Blessed are the dead which die in the Lord.'

Divine sympathy

Jesus wept.
John 11 v 35

When He saw the cave, and the stone, and the weeping friends, 'Jesus wept'. He wept because His heart was deeply touched. It was not feigned weeping, it was real. He knew that He was to raise him from the dead, and yet He wept because others wept. He wept as our example, to teach us to weep with one another. He wept to show what was in Him: 'For we have not an high-priest which cannot be touched with the feeling of our infirmities; but was in all points tempted like as we are, yet without sin. Let us therefore come boldly unto the throne of grace, that we may obtain mercy, and find grace to help in time of need' (Hebrews 4 vs. 15 &16.)

May *twenty-second*

What a friend we have in Jesus

Then said Martha unto Jesus, Lord, if thou hadst been here,
my brother had not died.
John 11 v 21

Learn that afflicting time is trying time. Affliction is like the furnace, it discovers the dross as well as the gold. Had all things gone on smoothly at Bethany, Martha and Mary had never known their sin and weakness; but now the furnace brought out the dross. Learn to guard against unbelief. Guard against presumption, making a Bible-promise for yourself, and leaning upon a word God has never spoken. Guard against prescribing your way to Christ, and limiting Him in His dealings. Guard against unbelief, believing only part of God's testimony. 'O foolish, and slow of heart to believe all that God hath spoken.' Remember, whatever your darkness may be, to carry your complaint to Jesus Himself.

May *twenty-third*

Open reward

But when thou doest alms, let not thy left hand know what thy right
hand doeth: That thine alms may be in secret: and thy Father which
seeth in secret himself shall reward thee openly.
Matthew 6 vs 3 & 4

If you give, hoping for something again, you will get nothing. You must give as a Christian gives, - cheerfully, liberally, and freely, hoping for nothing again; and then God will give you back good measure, pressed down. 'Give, and it shall be given you.'

May *twenty-fourth*

Experimental knowledge

... One thing I know, that , whereas I was blind, now I see.
John 9 v 25

The first thing that the Holy Spirit does when he is converting a soul is to give light: 'Ye were some time darkness, but now are ye light in the Lord.' He pours a flood of light into the unconverted soul, so that it sees itself. You remember at the first creation of the world, God said, 'Let there be light, and there was light.' So it is at the conversion of a soul. The first thing that the Holy Spirit does, is to give knowledge to let us see things as they are - to let us see ourselves as we are - heaven as it is - hell as it is. This light, brethren, too, is sanctifying light. 'Beholding as in a glass the glory of the Lord, we are changed into the same image, from glory to glory.' And this is saving light: 'For this is life eternal, to know thee, the only true God, and Jesus Christ whom thou hast sent.' You remember when Paul was converted, there were scales fell from his eyes, and he was enabled to see. Now this is just intended to show us what conversion is - it is as scales falling from the eyes - it is the giving of sight to the blind.

May *twenty-fifth*

Christ for us

But we see Jesus, who was made a little lower than the angels for the suffering of death, crowned with glory and honour; that he by the grace of God should taste death for every man.
Hebrews 2 v 9

Paul got such a view of the glory, brightness, and excellency of the way of salvation by Jesus, that it filled his whole heart. All other things sunk into littleness. Every mountain and hill was brought low, the crooked was made straight, the rough places smooth, and the glory of the Lord was revealed. As the rising sun makes all the stars disappear, so the rising of Christ upon his soul made everything else disappear. Jesus, suffering for us, filled his eye - filled his heart. He saw, believed, and was happy. Christ for us, answered all his need. From the Cross of Christ a ray of heavenly light flamed to his soul, filling him with light and joy unspeakable. He felt that God was glorified, and he was saved; he cleaved to the Lord with full purpose of heart.

May *twenty-sixth*

The better half of salvation

For this is the will of God, even your sanctification ...
I Thessalonians 4 v 3

Christ's work is not done with a soul when He has brought it to pardon - when He has washed it in His own Blood. Oh, no! the better half of salvation remains - His great work of sanctification remains.

May *twenty-seventh*

The anxious Christ

Then said Jesus unto the twelve, Will ye also go away?
John 6 v 67

When the crowd went away He did not cry after them - His soul was grieved, but He spoke not a word; but when His own believing disciples were in danger of being led away, He speaks to them: 'Will ye also go away?' - ye whom I have chosen - ye whom I have washed - ye whom I have sanctified and filled with hopes of glory - 'Will ye also go away?' Oh! see, Christians, how anxiously Christ watches over you. He is walking in the midst of the seven golden candlesticks, and His word is: 'I know thy works'. He watches the first decaying of the first love. He speaks aloud: 'Will ye also go away?'

May *twenty-eighth*

Put out the fire

And if Christ be in you, the body is dead because of sin; but the Spirit is life because of righteousness.
Romans 8 v 10

The only way to put out the fire, is to let in the water of the Spirit. Brethren, you think your planning will do it; but, no, there is nothing between you and deepest fall into sin, but the Spirit. Ah! many do not believe this; they say, my principles, my good name, my resolutions will keep me; but, Ah! brethren, remember there is no power but the Spirit dwelling in your soul, that will keep you from sin. There are many here may say, 'I will never go back to sin, I will never go back to the world' - and, I believe, you are honest in saying so; but stop a little, when your soul is far from Christ, when you do not have that sense of His presence that you now enjoy, and see what you will do. Ah! brethren, we are but worms, and they are the happiest worms who do least. Then, brethren, we must be sanctified entirely through the Spirit. If there be not an Almighty hand behind me, I cannot go to the Lord Jesus, I cannot keep myself from any sin.

Shut in or shut out
... And the door was shut
Matthew 25 v 10

The door of Christ stands wide open for a long time, but shuts at last. When Christ comes, the door will be shut. Now the door is open, and we are sent to invite you to come in. Soon it will be shut, and then you cannot. So it was at the flood. One hundred and twenty years the door of the ark stood wide open. Noah went forth, and preached everywhere, inviting men to come in. The Spirit strove with men. But they only mocked at the coming flood. At last the day came. Noah entered, and God shut him in. The door was shut. The flood came and carried them all away. So it will be with many here. The door is wide open now. Jesus says: 'I am the door: by me if any man enter in, he shall be saved, and shall go in and out, and find pasture.' Christ does not say, I was, or I will be, but, I am the door. At present any man may enter in. Soon Christ will come - like a thief - like a snare - like travail on a woman with child - and you shall not escape. Enter in at the strait gate.

Touched
For we have not an high priest which cannot be touched with
the feeling of our infirmities; but was in all points tempted like
as we are, yet without sin.
Hebrews 4 v 15

We have a merciful and faithful High Priest. He suffered being tempted, just that He might succour them that are tempted. The high priest of old not only offered sacrifice at the altar, - his work was not done when the lamb was consumed. He was to be a father to Israel. He carried all their names graven over his heart, - he went in and prayed for them within the veil. He came out and blessed the people, saying, 'The Lord bless thee and keep thee: The Lord make His face to shine upon thee, and be gracious unto thee: The Lord lift up his countenance upon thee, and give thee peace.'

So it is with the Lord Jesus. His work was not all done on Calvary. He that died for our sins lives to pray for us, - to help in every time of need.

He is still man on the right hand of God. He is still God, and therefore, by reason of His divinity, is present here this day as much as any of us. He knows your every sorrow, trial, difficulty; every half-hearted sigh He hears, and brings in notice thereof to His human heart at the right hand of God. His human heart is the same yesterday, to-day, and for ever; it pleads for you, thinks on you, plans deliverance for you.

Dear tempted brethren! go boldly to the throne of grace, to obtain mercy and find grace to help you in your time of need.

Perfect love

There is no fear in love; but perfect love casteth out fear: because fear hath torment. He that feareth is not made perfect in love.
I John 4 v 18

Twice God spake from heaven, and said, 'This is my beloved Son, in whom I am well pleased.' God perfectly loves His own Son. He sees infinite beauty in His person. God sees Himself manifested. He is infinitely pleased with His finished work. The infinite heart of the infinite God flows out in love towards our Lord Jesus Christ. And there is no fear in the bosom of Christ. All His fears are past. Once He said, 'While I suffer thy terrors I am distressed;' but now He is in perfect love, and perfect love casteth out fear: Hearken trembling souls! Here you may find rest to your souls. You do not need to live another hour under your tormenting fears. Jesus Christ has borne the wrath of which you are afraid. He now stands a refuge for the oppressed - a refuge in the time of trouble. Look to Christ, and you will find rest. Call upon the name of the Lord, and you will be delivered.

June

> "
>
> *The new element he brought into the pupit, or rather which he revived and used so much that it appeared new, was winsomeness.*
>
> "
>
> WILLIAM BLAIKIE

June *first*

The breathing of the new creature

O that my ways were directed to keep thy statutes!
Psalm 119 v 5

Brethren, this is a simple verse, but it is the breathing of the new creature; never did an old creature breathe this from his inmost soul. Can you say that? Do you breathe an entire devotedness to Him? Have you given up every sin for Him? Some of you may say, God forbid that I should part with every sin. It is but a little one; I cannot part with my money, I cannot part with my pleasures, I would come to the Lord's table. Well, you may come, but you come uninvited; nay, you come against the Master's will. None are invited but those who want complete devotedness to Him. Is it so with you? Some soul may say, 'O that my ways were directed to keep thy statutes.' I am vile, but thou knowest it will be heaven to me to be like thee. Is it so? Then the Master says, 'Come.' He says to you what He said to the disciples, 'Come and dine.' Amen.

June *second*

Hide behind him

To the praise of the glory of his grace, wherein he hath made us accepted in the beloved.
Ephesians 1 v 6

Jesus must be seen by the Father, instead of our guilty soul. You must leave self, and stand in your Elder Brother. Hide behind Him. Let the Father's eye fall on Him, not on you. This is what Jesus wants. He died to be a shelter for such as you. This is what the Father wants; for He is not willing that any should perish. If you are seen by the Father you must die. There is no help for it. But if Jesus appears for you - if you hide in His wounds, like the dove in the clefts of the rock - then the Father Himself loveth you.

Rest

... yea, saith the Spirit, that they may rest from their labours; and
their works do follow them.
Revelation 14 v 13

We shall 'rest from our labours.' We shall not rest from all work; we shall serve Him day and night in His temple. We shall not rest from our work, but from our labours. there will be no toil, no pain, in our work. We shall rest in our work. Oh, let this make you willing to depart, and make death look pleasant, and Heaven a home. It is a world of holy love, where we shall give free, full, unfettered, unwearied expression to our love for ever.

Is your watch keeping good time?

So teach us to number our days, that we may apply
our hearts unto wisdom.
Psalm 90 v12

I have found, by some experience, that in the country here my watch does not go so well as it used to do in town. By small and gradual changes I find it either gains or loses, and I am surprised to find myself different in time from all the world, and, what is worse, from the sun. The simple explanation is, that in town I met with a steeple in every street, and a good going clock upon it; and so any aberration in my watch were soon noticed and easily corrected. And just so I sometimes think it may be with that inner watch, whose hands point not to time but to eternity. By gradual and slow changes the wheels of my soul lag behind, or the springs of passion become too powerful; and I have no living timepiece with which I may amend my going. You will say that I always have the sun: And so it should be; but we may have many clouds which obscure the sun from our weak eyes.

Christ goes before

And when he putteth forth his own sheep, he goeth before them,
and the sheep follow him: for they know his voice.
John 10 v 4

In the countries of the east, brethren, you know that the shepherd goes before the sheep, and they follow him. When he says, 'Let us go to the well,' they follow him. When he says, 'Let us go down into that dark valley,' they go after him. So it is with Christ. Christ never asked a sheep to go where He never went Himself. He has borne all that He calls His sheep to bear. Christ went in a lower level of sorrow than you will be called to bear. Do not be alarmed then when you are called to suffer, you will not be called to go where He has not gone. Do not be afraid to put down your tender feet where He put down His. And it is still true that He goes before you. 'When thou passest through the waters, I will be with thee, and through the rivers, they shall not overflow thee; when thou walkest through the fire, thou shalt not be burned, neither shall the flame kindle upon thee.' Do not be afraid then when Christ is before you.

Secret prayer

But thou, when thou prayest, enter into thy closet, and when thou
hast shut thy door, pray to thy Father which is in secret; and thy
Father which seeth in secret shall reward thee openly.
Matthew 6 v 6

Christ loved secret prayer. Ah, you are no Christian, if you do not love secret prayer. O Brethren! a prayerless man is an unconverted man. Disguise it as you may; defend it as you can; explain it as you like; but a prayerless man is a Christless man.

A family quarrel

*And there was a strife between the herdmen of Abram's cattle and
the herdmen of Lot's cattle: and the Canaanite and the Perizzite
dwelled then in the land. And Abram said unto Lot, Let there
be no strife, I pray thee, between me and thee, and between
my herdmen and thy herdmen; for we be brethren.*
Genesis 13 vs 7 - 8

Domestic trials are not easy to bear. Most believers would like to go to heaven without a crook in their lot. I have no doubt that Jacob would have liked to have gone to heaven without the trial he had in the loss of Joseph; I have no doubt that David would have liked to have gone to heaven without the trial he had in the death of Absalom; and I have no doubt that Abraham would have liked to have gone to the better land without this strife breaking out between Lot and him. But it must not be.

The reason why domestic trials happen are - first, for the trial of our faith. Just as the jeweller puts the gold into the crucible, not to destroy the gold, but to separate it from the dross, so trials are intended by God to separate us from all dross. Another reason is to make us long for the better country. When God permits strife to rise in a believing family, it is to show you that this is not our home.

June *eighth*

Divine breathings

*But ye, beloved, building up yoursevles on your most holy faith,
praying in the Holy Ghost ...*
Jude v 20

When a believer prays, he is not alone - there are three with him: the Father seeing in secret, His ear open; the Son blotting out sin, and offering up the prayer; the Holy Ghost quickening and giving desires. There can be no true prayer without these three. Some people pray like a parrot, repeating words when the heart is far from God. Some pray without the Father. They do not feel. They are speaking to the back of their chair, or to the world, or to the empty air. Some pray without the Son. They come in their own name - in their own righteousness. That is the sacrifice of fools. Some pray without the Holy Ghost. These are not filled with divine breathings. Dear friends, if you would live, you must pray; and if you would pray with acceptance, you must pray to the Father in the name of Jesus, and by His Spirit quickening.

June *ninth*

For the elect's sake

Therefore I endure all things for the elect's sakes, that they may also obtain the salvation which is in Christ Jesus with eternal glory.
II Timothy 2 v 10

I sometimes feel brethren, that I would willingly lie down beneath the sod in the churchyard, and be forgotten and trampled on, if only you were friends of Christ.

June *tenth*

Everlasting love

Let your conversation be without covetousness; and be content with such things as ye have: for he hath said, I will never leave thee, nor forsake thee.
Hebrews 13 v 5

It is the word of the three-one God. You may take each of the persons of the Godhead, and apply this word to Him - 'I will never leave thee, nor forsake thee.' You may take it as the word of Immanuel. You remember what Christ said to His disciples - 'Lo, I am with you always, even unto the end of the world.' This is the same promise. Brethren, when the Lord Jesus comes to you, and covers you with His garment, and says, 'Fear not,' He will never forsake that soul. A mother may forsake - 'Can a woman forget her sucking child, that she should not have compassion on the son of her womb? Yea, she may forget; yet will I not forget thee.' Observe, brethren, that when once the Lord Jesus comes to a sinner to be His righteousness, He will never leave him - 'I am with you always.' Oh! it is this that makes Him a friend that sticketh closer than a brother. Why will He never leave us? The first reason is, His love is everlasting love. It is not like the love of a creature - it is unchangeable. Another reason is, He has died for that soul: He has borne all for that soul. Will he ever leave a soul that He has died for.

The same love

As the Father hath loved me, so have I loved you:
continue ye in my love.
John 15 v 9

The moment you become a child, the Father loves you. This is shown in what Christ said to Mary: 'I ascend unto my Father and to your Father, to my God and your God.' Christ here intimated, that we have the same love that he had. We have not got so much of the love of the Father as Christ, because He has got an infinite capacity; but it is the same love. The sun shines as much upon the daisy as it does upon the sunflower, though the sunflower is able to contain more. Christ plainly shows you that in the 17th chapter of John, where He prays that the same love may be in us that was in Him. O how much better is it then, to be under the love of God, than under the wrath of God!

Ordained

Ye have not chosen me, but I have chosen you, and ordained you,
that ye should go and bring forth fruit, and that your fruit
should remain: that whatsoever ye shall ask of the
Father in my name, he may give it to you.
John 15 v 16

This is a very humbling, and at the same time, a very blessed word to the true disciple. It was very humbling to the disciples to be told that they had not chosen Christ. Your wants were so many, your hearts were so hard, that ye have not chosen me. And yet it was exceedingly comforting to the disciples to be told that He had chosen them: 'Ye have not chosen me, but I have chosen you.' This showed them that His love was first with them - that He had a love that would make them holy: 'Ye have not chosen me, but I have chosen you, and ordained you, that ye should go and bring forth fruit, and that your fruit should remain.'

June *thirteenth*

Conversion

Repent ye therefore, and be converted, that your sins may be
blotted out, when the times of refreshing shall come from
the presence of the Lord;
Acts 3 v19

The conversion of a soul is by far the most remarkable event in the history of the world, although many of you do not care about it. It is the object that attracts the eyes of the holy angels to the spot where it takes place. It is the object which the Father's eye rests upon with tenderness and delight. This work in the soul is what brings greater glory to the Father, Son, and Spirit, than all the other works of God. It is far more wonderful than all the works of art. There is nothing that can equal it. Ah! brethren, if you think little of it, or laugh at it, how little have you of the mind of God.

June *fourteenth*

Christ's gift

And I give unto them eternal life; and they shall never perish,
neither shall any man pluck them out of my hand.
John 10 v 28

You know that the shepherd leads the sheep to a living well or to some gushing stream that flows between two rocks. So is it with Christ. Observe, it is said, 'I give unto them eternal life.' If you are one of Christ's flock you will never want. 'I give unto them eternal life.' What does this imply. It implies daily pardon. You know when the Queen sends a pardon to any condemned criminal, she is said to give the man his life. If you are Christ's you need daily pardon. If there is any sin separating between you and a loving God, you need it pardoned. It implies spiritual life. The life that Christ gives flows through the heart. If the Holy Spirit were to leave the heart, you would lose spiritual life. Thus David says, 'Take not thy Holy Spirit away from me. Restore unto me the joy of thy salvation, and uphold me with thy free Spirit.' Brethren, are you daily drinking of this loving water? Does it spring up within you? Ah! remember it is Christ's gift; 'I give unto them eternal life.'

This was His love

For he hath made him to be sin for us, who knew no sin; that we
might be made the righteousness of God in him.
II Corinthians 5 v 21

He hath made him to be sin for us. This is described in the Bible in a great many different ways. In the fifty-third chapter of Isaiah it is said, 'All we like sheep have gone astray, and the Lord hath laid on him the iniquity of us all'; and, verse 10, 'it pleased the Lord to bruise him,' etc. The same thing is described to us by Peter, in I Peter 2. v.24, 'Who his own self bare our sins in his own body on the tree.' But in this passage you will observe it is described in a far more dreadful manner. He heaped upon His Son all our sins until there was nothing but sin to be seen. He appeared all sin; nothing of His own beauty appeared; God took Him as if He were entirely made up of sin. You know that unconverted men are all sin. You say you have many good things about you; you are sometimes light in your walk, and take a glass occasionally; 'but I'm a good fellow after all.' Ah, you do not know that you are one mass of sin; your mind, your understanding, your affections, and your conscience. Brethren, look at the love of Christ, that He should be willing to be made sin for us, and this was His love.

God's wounded spirit

And grieve not the holy Spirit of God, whereby ye are sealed
unto the day of redemption.
Ephesians 4 v 30

Let me show you the holy friendship that subsists between the Holy Spirit and believer's soul. It is implied in the words, 'Grieve not the Holy Spirit.' It is only a friend we can grieve. If he was an enemy he would rejoice if we fell. And this shews that he is a true friend, because when we fall the Holy Spirit is grieved. It is quite true that the infinite God does not grieve in the same sense as we do, for that would imply that He was not infinitely happy; but it is quite as true that there is something analogous between His grief and ours.

June *seventeenth*

The work of the Spirit in the believer

Then he answered and spake unto me, saying, This is the word
of the Lord unto Zerubbabel, saying, Not by might, nor by
power, but by my spirit, saith the Lord of hosts.
Zechariah 4 v 6

This is the great work of the Spirit in you, to make you holy. 'Thy Spirit is good, lead me to the land of uprightness' God promises in Ezekiel 36 v. 27 'I will put my Spirit within you, and cause you to walk in my statutes, and ye shall keep my judgements and do them;' Now, as long as you lean on the Spirit for holiness, you and He are great friends, but the moment you cease to lean on Him, you grieve Him.

June *eighteenth*

A sweet mystery

As sorrowful, yet alway rejoicing; as poor, yet making many rich; as
having nothing, and yet possessing all things.
II Corinthians 6 v 10

The groans and triumphal song of a believer are not far separated, as you may see in Paul (Romans 7 vs. 24-25): 'O wretched man,' and 'I thank God,' all in one breath! David felt the same (see Psalm 73). At one verse he feels himself a fool and a beast in the sight of a holy God, and in the very next verses he is cleaving to Christ with a song of unspeakable joy (vs. 22-24). Ah! there is a sweet mystery here - bitter herbs along with our passover Lamb. It is sweet to see ourselves infinitely vile, that we may look to Jehovah our Righteousness, as all our way to the Father.

June *nineteenth*

A vale of tears

Surely it is meet to be said unto God, I have borne chastisement,
I will not offend any more: That which I see not teach thou me:
if I have done iniquity, I will do no more.
Job 34 vs 31 & 32

This world is a world of trouble: 'Man that is born of woman, is of few days, and full of trouble.' 'We dwell in cottages of clay, our foundation is in the dust, we are crushed before the moth,' (Job 4 v. 19). This world has sometimes been called 'a vale of tears.' Trials come into all your dwellings; the children of God are not excepted; there is a need be that you be in many temptations. 'Count it not strange when you fall into divers temptations, as though some strange thing happened unto you.' If this be so, of how great importance is it, that you and I be prepared to meet it. The darkest thunder cloud only covers the heavens for a time. 'Surely it is meet to be said unto God, I have borne chastisement. I will not offend any more: that which I see not, teach thou me; if I have done iniquity, I will do no more.'

June *twentieth*

Christian oneness

And this commandment have we from him, That he who loveth God love his brother also.
I John 4 v 21

The soul in Christ has many sweet companions - brothers and sisters in Christ Jesus. The soul that is united to the vine tree is united to all the branches: 'We know that we are passed from death unto life, because we love the brethren. 'I am a companion of all them that fear thee.'

June *twenty-first*

Christ within the veil

... and the ark of the covenant overlaid round about with gold, wherein was the golden pot that had manna ....
Hebrews 9 v 4

When God led Israel through the wilderness, 'He fed them with the corn of heaven; man did eat angels' food.' He rained down manna on them every morning for forty years. At that time God commanded them to preserve an omer of it (enough for one person) in a golden pot, 'that they may see the bread wherewith I have fed you in the wilderness' (Exodus 16 v. 32). Paul here tells us it was kept in a golden pot, beside the ark within the veil. There can be no doubt that the manna was a type of Jesus - the nourishment of His people. The bread of God is He which cometh down from heaven and giveth life unto the world. 'I am the bread of life' (John 6 v. 33). But the hidden manna represented Christ within the veil; and, accordingly, the promise to him that overcometh in the Church of Smyrna runs thus: 'To him that overcometh will I give to eat of the hidden manna' (Rev 2 v. 17). Jesus is not to be our food only in the the wilderness, but in eternity; we shall still feed on that hidden manna - that bread of God.

June *twenty-second*

The first sip of the cup of eternal bliss

And be ye kind one to another, tenderhearted, forgiving one another, even as God for Christ's sake hath forgiven you.
Ephesians 4 v 32

There is something very heavenly in these words. 'Son, be of good cheer, thy sins are forgiven thee.' Those of you who have be lieved on Christ, you are forgiven. 'As far as east is distant from the west, so far hath he removed our transgressions from us.' Your sins have been already forgiven, as many of you as have believed on Christ. If you really lay hold on Christ, sinner, tonight your sins will be forgiven thee. Oh, brethren, this is happiness - this is the first sip of the cup of eternal bliss - this is peace: 'Now the God of hope fill you with all joy and peace in believing.'

June *twenty-third*

Christ gave His life

I am the good shepherd: the good shepherd giveth his life for the sheep.
John 10 v11

Jacob was a good shepherd to Laban. You remember his care of the sheep; he says, 'That which was torn of beasts I brought not unto thee; I bare the loss of it; of my hand didst thou require it, whether stolen by day or stolen by night.' etc.,(Gen. 31 vs 39 - 40). But he did not give his life for the sheep. David was a good shepherd. You remember when a lion and a bear came and took away the sheep, that he went after it and rescued it, and slew both the lion and the bear; (I Samuel 17 v. 35). But David did not give his life for the sheep; but Christ gave His life. The sentence was written against the sheep, 'Thou shalt die;' - Christ came between and died for them.

June *twenty-fourth*

A Gospel ministry

For we preach not ourselves, but Christ Jesus the Lord; and ourselves your servants for Jesus' sake.
II Corinthians 4 v 5

Many men preach themselves - they preach their own theories. Many before the days of the apostles did this - they taught their own fancies. But when the apostles came they took a very different manner. Witness John the Baptist - 'Behold the Lamb of God that taketh away the sin of the world.' So the apostles; they said, 'We are witnesses of all things which he did both in the land of the Jews and in Jerusalem; whom they slew and hanged on a tree.' And then you remember Philip when he went down to Samaria, 'he preached Christ unto them.' And this is exactly what John says in his 1st Epistle, 'That which we have seen and heard declare we unto you.' This is the very beginning, middle, and end of a gospel ministry. And looking back on the five years we have been together, I think I can lay my hand upon my heart, and feebly think this is what I have done. And why should we do this? Because it is the most awakening truth in the world. One evening lately, I was passing by a building and I heard a man speaking, who seemed in earnest. I stopped and listened - he was preaching about laws and politics. I said that man may preach to the day of judgement, but he will never make the people holy. But we preach Christ Jesus the Lord, that you may be made holy.

June *twenty-fifth*

The body of death

I thank God through Jesus Christ our Lord. So then with the mind I myself serve the law of God; but with the flesh the law of sin.
Romans 7 v 25

In ancient times, some of the tyrants used to chain their prisoners to a dead body; so that, wherever the prisoner wandered, he had to drag a putrid carcass after him. It is believed that Paul here alludes to this inhuman practice. His old man he felt a noisome, putrid carcass, which he was continually dragging about with him. His piercing desire is to be freed from it. Who shall deliver us? You remember once, when God allowed a thorn in the flesh to torment His servant, - a messenger of Satan to buffet him, - Paul was driven to his knees. 'I besought the Lord thrice, that it might depart from me.' Oh, this is the true make of God's children! The world has an old nature; they are all old men together. But it does not drive them to their knees. How is it with you, dear souls? Does corruption felt within drive you to the throne of grace? Does it make you call on the name of the Lord? Does it make you like the man coming at midnight for three loaves? Does it make you like the Canaanitish woman, crying after Jesus? Ah, remember, if lust can work in your heart, and you lie down contented with it, you are none of Christ's!

June *twenty-sixth*

Conquerors

Nay, in all these things we are more than conquerors through him that loved us.
Romans 8 v 37

Truly we are more than conquerors through Him that loved us; for we can give thanks before the fight is done. Yes, even in the thickest of the battle we can look up to Jesus, and cry, Thanks to God. The moment a soul, groaning under corruption, rests the eye on Jesus, that moment his groans are changed into songs of praise. In Jesus you discover a fountain to wash away the guilt of all your sin. In Jesus you discover grace sufficient for you, - grace to hold you up to the end, - and a sure promise that sin shall soon be rooted out altogether. 'Fear not, I have redeemed thee. I have called thee by My name; thou art Mine.' Ah, this turns our groans into songs of praise! How often a psalm begins with groans and ends with praises! This is the daily experience of all the Lord's people. Is it yours? Try yourselves by this. Oh, if you know not the believer's song of praise, you will never cast your crowns with them at the feet of Jesus! Dear believers, be content to glory in your infirmities, that the power of Christ may rest upon you. Glory, glory, glory to the Lamb!

Lean hard

Who is this that cometh up from the wilderness, leaning
upon her beloved?
Song of Solomon 8 v 5

I t is very observable that there is none here but the bride and her beloved in a vast wilderness. She is not leaning upon Him with one arm, and upon somebody else with the other; but she is leaning upon Him alone. So is it with the soul taught of God; it feels alone with Christ in this world; it leans as entirely upon Christ as if there were no other being in the universe. She leans all her weight upon her husband. When a person has beem saved from drowning, they lean all their weight upon their deliverer. When the lost sheep was found, He took it upon His shoulder. You must be content then to lean all your weight upon Christ. Cast the burden of temporal things upon Him. Cast the care of your soul upon Him. If God be for us, who can be against us? They that wait upon the Lord shall renew their strength. The eagle soars so directly upward, that poets have fancied it was aiming at the sun. So does the soul that waits on Christ.

Be not weary in well doing

He that goeth forth and weepeth, bearing precious seed, shall doubt-
less come again with rejoicing, bringing his sheaves with him.
Psalm 126 v 6

G o to the field when the seed has been covered in. Do you see any marks of growing? No, not a green speck. Still the work in going on. Have patience; weary not in well-doing. Be instant in prayer. God will be faithful to His promise. 'His word shall not return unto Him void.'

What God will not give

I am the Lord: that is my name: and my glory will I not
give to another, neither my praise to graven images.
Isaiah 42 v 8

If Christ has been made to rise on your soul, happy are you. You were sometime darkness, but now you are light in the Lord. Walk as children of the light. See who did it, and give him the praise. It is the Lord. God gave Christ to be a light to thy soul. Give Him, and Him alone, the glory. 'My glory will I not give to another.' (1) Do not give the praise to yourself. Do not say, my own wisdom or my own prayers have gotten me this. It was all undeserved mercy to the chief of sinners. 'My glory will I not give to another.' (2) Do not give the glory to ministers. They are often the instruments of bringing souls to Christ, but they cannot make Christ arise on the soul, any more than they can make the sun to rise on the earth. We can point to the sun, though we cannot make it rise; so, we can point you to Christ, but cannot make Him rise on your soul. The work is God's, and He will have the glory. I believe the work is greatly hindered amongst us from the cause mentioned.

Plead with God to fulfil His word, that Christ may be a light to the nations. It is as easy with God to make Christ rise on many souls as upon one. Show Him that it is for His glory that a nation be born in a day. Give Him no rest till he pour down the Spirit on all our families, till there be a great looking unto Jesus, and rejoicing in Him. Take thine own glory, O Lord; give it to no other, neither thy praise to graven images.

June *thirtieth*

Where is your faith?

And he saith unto them, Why are ye fearful, O ye of little faith?
Then he arose, and rebuked the winds and the sea; and there
was a great calm.
Matthew 8 v 26

One evening Christ gave commandment on the Sea of Galilee to depart to 'the other side'; and as they sailed He fell asleep. Here was a simple word of promise to hold by in the storm. But when the storm came down, and the waves covered the ship, they cried, 'Master, save us; we perish.' And He said: 'Where is your faith?' By that trial the faith of the disciples was greatly increased ever after. So it is with all trials of faith. When God gives a promise, He always tries our faith. Just as the roots of trees take firmer hold when they are contending with the wind, so faith takes a firmer hold when it struggles with adverse appearances.

July

> "
>
> *Read McCheyne's Memoirs ... it is the story of the life of a man who walked with God.*
>
> "
>
> C. H. SPURGEON

July *first*

Follow Jesus

And as Jesus passed forth from thence, he saw a man,
named Matthew, sitting at the receipt of custom:
and he saith unto him, Follow me. And he
arose, and followed him.
Matthew 9 v 9

Matthew was sitting at the receipt of custom when Jesus passed by. How wonderful is the grace of the Lord Jesus. Some of you may be living in an evil calling, or in your sins. Look up, the Lord Jesus this night may turn His eye upon you.

A simple word is blessed - 'Follow me'. No argument. It is probable he had heard of Christ, heard Him preach, seen the preceding miracle; still he was at his old trade, till Jesus said, 'Follow me.' A little word reached his heart. We often make great mistakes- often make use of long arguments to bring people to Christ. Often we make use of long high-sounding words, and expect them to be blessed; whereas it is the simple exhibition of Christ.

July *second*

We believe

And we believe and are sure that thou art that Christ,
the Son of the living God.
John 6 v 69

We believe and are sure that thou art that Christ, the Son of the living God. Ah! it is this that rivets the believing soul to Christ - the certain conviction that Christ is a divine Saviour. If Christ were only a man like ourselves, then how could He be a surety for us? He might suffer in the stead of one man, but how could He suffer in the stead of thousands? Ah! but I believe and am sure that He is the Son of the living God, and therefore I know He is a sufficient surety for me. To whom else can I go for pardon? If Christ were only a man like ourselves, then how could He dwell in us, or give the Spirit to abide with us for ever? But we believe and are sure that He is that Christ, the Son of the living God, and therefore we know He is able to dwell in us, and put the Spirit in us for ever. To whom, then, can I go for a new heart but unto Christ? O dear brethren! have you been thus taught? Then blessed are ye, 'for flesh and blood hath not revealed it unto you, but my Father which is in heaven.' Hold fast by this sure faith for you cannot be too sure; and then you will never, never go away from Christ.

July *third*

Christ's intercession

Who is he that condemneth? It is Christ that died, yea rather, that is risen again, who is even at the right hand of God, who also maketh intercession for us.
Romans 8 v 34

f I could hear Christ praying for me in the next room, I would not fear a million enemies. Yet the distance makes no difference: He is praying for me.

July *fourth*

The Holy Scriptures

Search the scriptures; for in them ye think ye have eternal life: and they are they which testify of me.
John 5 v 39

ne gem from that ocean is worth all the pebbles of earthly streams.

Laden with guilt and full of fears,
I fly to Thee, my Lord,
And not a glimpse of hope appears,
But in the written word.

The volume of my Father's grace
Does all my griefs assuage;
Here I behold my Saviour's face
Almost in every page?

This is the field where hidden lies
The pearl of price unknown:
The merchant is divinely wise
Who makes the pearl his own.

Here consecrated water flows,
To quench my thirst of sin;
Here the fair tree of knowledge grows,
Nor danger dwells therein.

This is the judge that ends the strife,
Where wit and reason fail:
My guide to everlasting life,
Through all this gloomy vale.

O may thy counsels, mighty God,
My roving feet command;
Nor I forsake the happy road
That leads to thy right hand.

~ *Robert Murray McCheyne*

July *fifth*

Humility

Humble yourselves in the sight of the Lord, and he shall lift you up.
James 4 v 10

Oh for true, unfeigned humility! I know I have cause to be humble; and yet I do not know one half of the cause. I know I am proud; and yet I do not know the half of that pride.

July *sixth*

Nothing to spare

But the wise answered, saying, Not so; lest there be not enough for us and you: but go ye rather to them that sell, and buy for yourselves.
Matthew 25 v 9

It pleases God to use the godly as instruments, but he has not given them to be fountains of grace: 'I have planted, Apollos watered; but God gave the increase' (1 Corinthians 3:6). Rachel said to Jacob: 'Give me children, or else I die. And Jacob's anger was kindled against Rachel: and he said, Am I in God's stead?'(Genesis 30:1,2).

So grace is not in the hand of man. Those who receive Christ 'are born, not of blood, nor of the will of the flesh, nor of the will of man, but of God' (John 1:13). It is in vain, then, that you look to the means to give saving grace to your soul. The axe can hew without the hand of the forester. The pitcher that carries water is not the well. It will be in vain that you apply to God's children in that awful day. Go to Jesus now. The righteous scarcely are saved. Every child of God gets just so much grace as will carry him to heaven, and no more. Even now every child of God feels that he has nothing to spare. He has not too much of the Holy Spirit, helping him to pray, to mourn over sin, to love Christ. In time of temptation a believer feels as if he had nothing of the Holy Spirit. He has more need to receive, than ability to give away.

When Christ shall come in that solemn hour, he will feel that he has none to spare.

July *seventh*

Different ways

Be ye not unequally yoked together with unbelievers: for what fellowship hath righteousness with unrighteousness? and what communion hath light with an infidel?
II Corinthians 6 v 14

Can two walk together except they be agreed? It is impossible that two souls can be happy together if they love opposite things. It is like two bullocks in the yoke drawing different ways. Hence the deep wisdom of the command which forbids God's children to intermarry with the world. What fellowship hath light with darkness? In the same way with Christ's bride, she must be of one mind with him, if she would enter in with him to the marriage.

Suppose one of you who has an old heart were to be admitted with Christ to the marriage. Your heart is enmity to God, you hate God's people, the Sabbath is a weariness, you serve divers lusts and pleasures. The Lamb that is in the midst of the throne would lead you, and God would wipe away tears from your eyes. But you hate God and the Lamb. How could you be happy there? None but God's children or companions (psalm-singing hypocrites, as you used to call them) - could you be happy with them? An eternal Sabbath! My highest notion of heaven is an eternal Sabbath with Christ. Could you be happy? Could you enjoy it? Ah, my friends, there shall in no wise enter in any that defileth, and that maketh or loveth a lie. If you are still unborn again, you are not ready.

July *eighth*

When weakness is strength

Therefore I take pleasure in infirmities, in reproaches,
in necessities, in persecutions, in distresses for Christ's sake:
for when I am weak, then am I strong.
II Corinthians 12 v 10

When the believer is weakest, then is he strongest. The child that knows most its utter feebleness, entrusts itself most completely into the mother's arms. The young eagle that knows, by many a fall, its own inability to fly, yields itself to be carried on the mother's mighty wing. When it is weak, then it is strong; and just so the believer when he has found out, by repeated falls, his own utter feebleness, clings, with simplest faith, to the arm of the Saviour and leans on his Beloved, coming up out of the wilderness, and hears with joy the words: 'My grace is sufficient for thee; my strength is made perfect in weakness.'

July *ninth*

The father's gift

I the Lord have called thee in righteousness, and will hold thine
hand, and will keep thee, and give thee for a covenant of
the people, for a light of the Gentiles;
Isaiah 42 v 6

God so loved the world, that he gave his only Son, that whosoever believeth on him should not perish.' 'Herein is love; not that we loved God.' God not only provided the Saviour, and upheld Him, but He gave Him - gave Him away, to be a covenant Saviour of the people, and a light to lighten the Gentiles. When Abraham bound his son Isaac upon the altar and lifted up the knife to strike, this was giving away his son at the command of God, This is just what God did. He took His son out of His bosom, and gave Him away to be bound, to be a covenant Saviour of the people. There are not more wonderful words in the whole Bible than these: 'I will give thee.' 'God spared not his own Son, but freely delivered him up to the death for us all.' The Son was infinitely dear to the Father. God cannot but love that which is perfectly holy and beautiful. Now, such was Christ. From all eternity there had been the outgoings of love and infinite admiration from the bosom of the Father towards His well-beloved Son. Canst thou part with me? Canst thou give me up to the garden and the cross? 'I will give thee.' Sinners were infinitely vile in the sight of the Father. God cannot but hate that which is enmity and rebellion to Himself. 'He is of purer eyes than to behold iniquity.' How loathsome and hateful this world must have been in His eyes, where every heart was enmity against him! Canst thou give me up for such sinners, for the sake of such vile worms? 'Yes, I will give thee.'

July *tenth*

Taught by the Spirit

Trust in the Lord with all thine heart; and lean not unto thine own understanding.
Proverbs 3 v 5

Well may every soul that is untaught by the Spirit of God exclaim: 'This is a hard saying, who can hear it?' And, indeed, there is perhaps no truth that calls forth more of the indignant opposition of the world than this blessed one, that they who trust in the Lord with all their heart do not lean to their own understanding. The understanding, here, plainly includes all the observing, knowing, and judging faculties of the mind, by which men ordinarily guide themselves in the world; and, accordingly, it is with no slight appearance of reasonableness that the world should brand with the name of fanatics a peculiar set of men, who dare to say that they are not to lean upon these faculties, to guide them in their every-day walk and conversation.

But surely it might do something to moderate, at least, the opposition of the world (if they would but listen to us), to tell them that we never refuse to be guided by the understanding, although we altogether refuse to lean upon it. Every enlightened believer, however implicitly he depends upon the breathing of the Holy Ghost, without whose almighty breathing he knows that his understanding would be but a vain and useless machine, leading him into darkness, and into light, yet follows the guidance of the understanding as scrupulously and as religiously as any unconverted man is able to do. Therefore, it ought never to be said, by any man who has a regard for truth, that the believer in Jesus casts aside the use of his understanding, and looks for miraculous guidance from on high. The truth is this, that he trusts in a divine power enlightening the understanding, and he therefore follows the dictates of the understanding more religiously than any other man.

July *eleventh*

Love for eternity

So are the paths of all that forget God; and the
hypocrite's hope shall perish:
Job 8 v 13

A hypocrite lives for time. This was all Judas lived for if he could pass off for a while as a true disciple, if he could keep up appearances for a time, if he could indulge his lusts, and yet be esteemed a believer, and a true apostle. He tried to keep up appearances to the last. So Demas wanted to deceive Paul for this life - to be thought a brother. Alas, how many of you are thus foolish! Living so as to keep up an appearance of being a Christian for a little time, though you know that you are living in positive sin, and that you will be discovered before the world in a short time. You only are truly wise who live for eternity, who live as you shall wish you had done when you come to die.

July *twelfth*

Such is your declaration

For as often as ye eat this bread, and drink this cup, ye do
shew the Lord's death till he come.
I Corinthians 1 v 26

The bride in the Song of Solomon says: 'As the apple tree among the trees of the wood, so is my beloved among the sons. I sat down under his shadow with great delight, and his fruit was sweet to my taste.' So do you say in coming to the Lord's table: I have found rest in the shade of Christ, His fruit is sweet to me; His way of pardon, His Spirit, His commands all are sweet to my taste.

When the maniac had the devils cast out, he sat at the feet of Jesus clothed, and in his right mind. Once he bade Jesus depart: 'What have I to do with thee?' Now Christ is all. Such is your declaration at the Lord's Table.

When Paul was an unconverted man, he was a blasphemer - he breathed out threatenings. But when he got a taste of Jesus, he said, 'I count all things but loss for the excellency of the knowledge of Christ Jesus my Lord.' Such is your declaration in taking that bread and wine.

Can you truly say that you have found the treasure, that you have sold all for it, that you have sat down under the shade of that apple tree, and that you delight in His holy fruit; that you were once far from Christ, but now sitting at His feet; that you now preach the faith which once you destroyed - that, like Paul, you glory only in the cross of Christ? Can you say, in the sight of God, that Christ is your manna, your sweet food, your peace, your all? Then you are welcome to the Lord's table. 'Eat, O friends; drink, yea, drink abundantly, O beloved.'

July *thirteenth*

He will come

For yet a little while, and he that shall come will come,
and will not tarry.
Hebrews 10 v 37

Christ is at this moment gathering a people from among the Gentiles. He is building up the great temple of the Lord, adding stone to stone. He cannot come till this is done. When all this is done, then He will come, and put on the top-stone, with shoutings of 'Grace, grace unto it.' He told Paul to remain and preach at Corinth: 'For I have much people in this city.' For the same reason He makes His ministers remain and preach on; for He has much people still. When He comes, those that are ready will enter in with Him to the marriage, and the door will be shut. There are, no doubt, many elect ones, many that were given Him by the Father.

July *fourteenth*

The reason why

When Jesus heard that, he said, This sickness is not unto death, but
for the glory of God, that the Son of God might be glorified thereby.
John 11 v 4

Some might ask, Why, then, was Lazarus sick? The reason: 'For the glory of God.' Christ was thereby in an eminent manner made known. First, His amazing love to His own was seen, when He wept at the grave. Second, His power to raise the dead. He was shown to be the Resurrection and the Life when He cried, 'Lazarus, come forth.'

Christ was far more glorified than if Lazarus had not been sick and died. So in all the sufferings of God's people. Sometimes a child of God says: Lord, what wilt Thou have me to do? I will teach, preach, do great things for Thee. Sometimes the answer is, Thou shalt suffer for my sake.

It shows the power of Christ's blood, when it gives peace in an hour of trouble, when it can make happy in sickness, poverty, persecution and death. Do not be surprised if you suffer, but glorify God.

It brings out graces that cannot be seen in a time of health. It is the treading of the grapes that brings out the sweet juices of the vine; so it is affliction that draws forth submission, weanedness from the world, and complete rest in God. Use afflictions while you have them.

July *fifteenth*

The stream of grace

He that believeth on me, as the scripture hath said, out of his belly
shall flow rivers of living water.
John 7 v 38

The Holy Spirit is an imperishable stream. It is not like those rivers of which you have heard, which flow through barren sands till they sink into the earth and disappear. Not so the stream of grace. When it flows from Jesus Christ, it flows into many a barren heart; but it is never lost there. It appears again - it flows forth from that heart in rivers of living water. When a soul is brought to believe on Jesus, and to drink in the Spirit, it often appears as if the Spirit were lost in that soul. The stream flows into such a barren heart, that it is long before it makes its appearance; but it is never lost. The Scripture must be fulfilled: 'He that believeth on me, out of his belly shall flow rivers of living water.'

July *sixteenth*

Study holiness

But as he which hath called you is holy, so be ye holy
in all manner of conversation;
I Peter 1 v 15

Seek daily likeness to Jesus. We are not justified by our sanctification; and yet without sanctification we cannot have abiding peace or communion. We are justified entirely by the doing and dying of the Lord Jesus; and yet, when justified, He will change us into His image; so that the longer we are justified we should be the more sanctified. Study holiness, if you would have peace now, and be found of Christ in peace. The holiest believers are evermore the happiest.

The Lord our shepherd

The Lord is my shepherd; I shall not want.
Psalm 23 v1

I t is exceedingly interesting to know the many names by which Christ calls Himself in the Bible. These are above one hundred, I think one hundred and seven. He calls Himself a rose, 'I am the rose of Sharon,' and a lily, 'I am the lily of the valley.' The reason why He has so many names is that one name would not describe Him; He has so many offices that one name would not explain them; nay all of them put together do not, for Paul said, 'Unto me who am less than the least of all saints is this grace given, that I might preach among the Gentiles the unsearchable riches of Christ.' Of all the names given, that of a shepherd is the sweetest.

Hallelujah! What a Saviour

For he hath made him to be sin for us, who knew no sin; that we might be made the righteousness of God in him.
I Corinthians 5 v 21

Y ou know brethren, that the pardon and justification of sinners is spoken of in different ways in the Bible. In Romans 3 v. 24, it is said, 'Being justified freely by his grace, through the redemption that is in Christ Jesus.' Again, in Romans 5 v. 19, 'For as by one man's disobedience many were made sinners, so by the obedience of one shall many be made righteous.'

But observe that these words express it more fully. I think it means that those of you who have come to the Lord Jesus, His righteousness shall cover you, that you will appear one mass of righteousness. And, brethren, observe what a provision is here for sinners - for the chief of sinners; for it matters not how great of how small a sinner you are; if you come to Christ, His righteousness will cover you so that none of your sin will be seen. O my friends, is not this a gospel worth preaching? May you now say as Luther used to do, 'Thou art made my sin, and I am made thy righteousness.'

July *nineteenth*

Lost opportunity

And the King shall answer and say unto them, Verily I say unto you, Inasmuch as ye have done it into one of the least of these my brethren, ye have done it unto me.
Matthew 25 v 40

Many Christians are content to be Christians for themselves - to hug the gospel to themselves, to sit in their own room, and feast upon it alone. This did not Christ. It is true He loved much to be alone. He once said to His disciples: 'Come into a desert place, and rest a while.' He often spent the whole night in prayer on the lone mountain-side; but it is as true that He went about continually. He went and saw, and then He had compassion. He did not hide Himself from His own flesh. You should be

Christ-like. Your word should be: 'Go and see.' You should go and see the poor; and then you will feel for them. Remember what Jesus said to all His people: 'I was sick, and in prison. and ye visited me.' Be not deceived, my dear friends; it is easy to give a cold pittance of charity at the church door, and to think that that is the religion of Jesus. But, 'Pure religion and undefiled, before God and the Father is this, to visit the fatherless and widows in their affliction, and to keep yourself unspotted from the world.'

July *twentieth*

Christ's garden

My beloved is gone down into his garden, to the beds of spices, to feed in the gardens, and to gather lilies.
Song of Soloman 6 v 2

When God made man at the first, He planted a garden east ward in Eden; and out of the ground made the Lord God to grow evey tree that is pleasant to the sight and good for food - the tree of life also, in the midst of the garden. And the Lord God took the man and put him into the garden of Eden, to dress and to keep it. That garden was a sweet type of the delight of Adam's soul; and there, day by day, he heard the voice of God walking in the garden, in the cool of the day. When Adam fell, God drove him out of the garden into this bleak world, covered with thorns and thistles, to earn his bread by the sweat of his brow. Man no more walked with God in a garden of delights.

But when a sinner is brought to Christ, he is brought into Christ's garden: 'We who believe, do enter into rest.' He says: 'I sat down under his shadow with great delight, and his fruit was sweet to my taste.' He becomes one that dwells in the gardens. True, he is one coming up from the wilderness. This world is a wilderness to the believer - full of pain, sickness, sighing, death - a world that crucified his Lord, and persecutes him - a cold, unbelieving, ungodly world. Still the soul dwells in the gardens; 'His soul shall dwell at ease.' True, a believer has his times of desertion, and clouds, and doubts, and deep waters. At such times, his cry is: 'O wretched man!' Still when his eye rests on Jesus, his soul dwells in a garden of delights.

July *twenty-first*

In time of death

The last enemy that shall be destroyed is death.
I Corinthians 15 v 26

Few ever think of dying till dying comes. The last enemy that shall be overcome is Death; and an awful enemy he is. We go alone. No earthly friend goes with us. We never went the way before. It is all strange and new. The results are eternal. If we have not rightly believed, it is too late to mend. These are some of the solemn thoughts that overshadow the soul. What can give peace? None but Jesus; the sight of Jesus as a Redeemer, the same yesterday, today, and forever; the same sight we got when first we knew the Lord, when first He chose us and we chose Him, when first He said, 'Seek ye my face,' and we said to Him, 'Thy face, Lord, shall we seek.' To see Him as a God of truth, the Lord that changes not, the unchanging One, the same Jesus; thus to see Him and to cry, 'Into thy hands I commit my spirit' - this is peace.

July *twenty-second*

Saints known

I am the good shepherd, and know my sheep, and am known of mine.
As the Father knoweth me, even so know I the Father: and I lay
down my life for the sheep.
John 10 vs 14 -15

The Father knew the Son from all eternity: 'Then I was by him as one brought up with him: and I was daily his delight, rejoicing always before him' (Proverbs 8. v. 30). He was in the bosom of the Father. So did this good shepherd know his sheep from all eternity: 'Chosen before the foundation of the world.'

The Father knew the Son with a knowledge of most perfect delight and love: 'I was daily his delight.' At his baptism, a voice from heaven was heard saying: 'This is my beloved Son, in whom I am well pleased' (Matthew 3 v. 17). So does Christ know his sheep: 'Thou art all fair, my love; there is no spot in thee;' 'The King is held in the galleries;' 'How fair and how pleasant art thou, O love, for delights!' 'Turn away thine eyes from me, for they have overcome me.'

The Father knew the Son through all his sufferings. So Christ knows his sheep: 'I know their sorrows;' 'In all their afflictions, he was afflicted.' He knows their decays: 'I know thy works, that thou art neither cold nor hot.'

The Father will know the Son to all eternity; and so the Son will know his sheep for ever and ever. They shall soon 'hunger no more, neither thirst any more; neither shall the sun light on them, nor any heat' (Revelation 7 v. 16).

July *twenty-third*

Good news

For ye know the grace of our Lord Jesus Christ, that , though he
was rich, yet for your sakes he became poor, that ye through
his poverty might be rich.
II Corinthians 8 v 9

Corinth was one of the most wicked cities that ever was on the face of the world. It lay between two seas; so that luxury came flowing in from the east and from the west. These Corinthians had been saved from the deepest abominations, as you learn from I Corinthians 6 v. 11: 'Such were some of you'; and yet it was for the sake of such that the Lord of glory became poor - 'For your sakes'. In like manner, Paul writing to the Romans, says: 'When we were without strength, in due time Christ died for the ungodly' (5:6). Ah! see what names are here given to those for whom Christ died: without strength - unable to believe, or to think a right thought; ungodly -living as if there were no God; sinners - breaking God's holy law; enemies -hating and opposing a holy God of love.

Oh, brethren! this is good news for the most wicked of men. Are there some of you who feel that you are like a beast before God, or all over sin. like a devil? Some of you have lived in the abominations of Corinth. Some of you are like the Romans - without strength, ungodly, sinners, enemies; yet for your sakes Christ became poor. He left glory for souls as vile as you. He left the songs of angels, the love of his Father, and the glories of heaven for just such wretches as you and me. He died for the ungodly. So not be afraid, sinners, to lay hold upon him. It was for your sakes he came. He will not, he cannot cast you out.

July *twenty-fourth*

Heaven began on earth

Unto Him that loved us, and washed us from our sins in His own blood, and hath made us kings and priests unto God and His Father; to Him be glory and dominion for ever and ever. Amen.
Revelation 1 vs 5-6

Some have thought this to be one of the songs of heaven. They have thought that, even before John's eye penetrated into the wonders of the upper world, its song of joy and ecstasy burst upon his ear - 'Unto Him that loved us.' This is evidently a mistake. It is the song of John - banished - poor - in trial and tribulation - an exiled man upon a lonely rock of the sea - a man who had his heaven begun on earth: 'Unto Him that loved us.' It has got the fragrance and melody of heaven about it. Believers, do not fear a suffering lot. Do not fear though you be taken to a lone sick-bed, or a lone rock dashed by the eternal waves of ocean. If you really know Jesus, and have tasted and seen the grace that is in Christ, you may begin the song now, 'Unto Him that loved us'.

July *twenty-fifth*

'Abba, Father'

And because ye are sons, God hath sent forth the Spirit of his Son
into your hearts, crying, Abba, Father.
Galations 4 v 6

No natural man cries, 'Abba'. It is not the cry of nature. Children cry 'Father' to their earthly parents. It is one of the first things they learn. They do not thus call upon God; but when one comes to Christ, and feels the Father's smile, the Father's arms, the Father's love, he cries 'Abba'.

Often it is little more than a cry. Many of God's children are not fluent in prayer. They have not many words.

Often they can only look up, and cry, 'Father'. A soul in Christ can cry, 'Father!' This runs through all he says to God, 'Abba'. 'In the multitude of words there wanteth ot sin,' but this one word is the believer's prayer, 'Abba'.

July *twenty-sixth*

Complete assurance

Consider the Apostle and High Priest of our profession, Christ Jesus.
Hebrews 3 v 1

Oh, brethren, could you and I pass this day through these heavens, and see what is now going on in the sanctuary above, - could you see what the child of God now sees who died last night, - could you see the Lamb with the scars of His five deep wounds in the very midst of the throne, surrounded by all the odours, - could you see the many angels round about the throne, whose number is ten thousand times ten thousand, and thousands of thousands, all singing, 'Worthy is the Lamb that was slain,' - and were one of these angels to tell you, 'This is He that undertook the cause of lost sinners; He undertook to be the second Adam, - the man in their stead; and lo! there He is upon the throne of heaven; - consider Him, - look long and earnestly upon His wounds - upon His glory, - and tell me, do you think it would be safe to trust Him? Do you think His sufferings and obedience will have been enough? - Yes, yes, every soul exclaims, Lord, it is enough! Lord, stay thy hand! Show me no more, for I can bear no more. Oh, rather let me ever stand and gaze upon the almighty, all-worthy, all-divine Saviour, till my soul drink in complete assurance that His work undertaken for sinners is a finished work! Yes, though the sins of all the world were on my one wicked head, still I could not doubt that His work is complete, and that I am quite safe when I believe in Him.

July *twenty-seventh*

Turn your eyes upon Jesus

Looking unto Jesus the author and finisher of our faith;who for the joy that was set before him endured the cross, desposong the shame,and is set down at the right hand of the throne of God.
Hebrews 12 v 2

Keep looking then to Jesus dear soul, and you will have the peace that passeth all understanding. Whenever Satan accuses you, send him to the stripes of Jesus.

July *twenty-eighth*

A spiritual mind

But we have the mind of Christ.
I Corinthians 2 v 16

Now, every believer has the mind of Christ formed in him. He thinks as Christ does: 'This is the spirit of a sound mind' (II Timothy 1v. 7). This is being of the same mind in the Lord. I do not mean that a believer has the same all-seeing mind, the same infallible judgement concerning everything, as Christ has; but up to his light he sees things as Christ does.

He sees sin as Christ does. Christ sees sin to be evil and bitter. He sees it to be filthy and abominable, its pleasures all a delusion. He sees it to be awfully dangerous. He sees the inseparable connection between sin and suffering. So does a believer.

He sees the gospel as Christ does. Christ sees amazing glory in the gospel, the way of salvation which He Himself has wrought out. It appears a most complete salvation to Him, most free, most glorifying to God and happy for man. So does the believer.

He sees the world as Christ does. Christ knows what is in man. He looked on this world as vanity compared with the smile of His Father. Its riches, its honours, its pleasures, appeared not worth a sigh. He saw it passing away. So does the believer.

He sees time as Christ did. 'I must work the works of him that sent me, while it is day: the night cometh when no man can work' - 'I come quickly.' So does a believer look at time.

He sees eternity as Christ does. Christ looked at everything in the light of eternity. 'In my Father's house are many mansions.' Everything is valuable in Christ's eyes, only as it bears on eternity. So with believers.

July *twenty-ninth*

God is stronger than Satan

Ye are of God , little children, and have overcome them: because greater is he that is in you, than he that is in the world.
I John 4 v 4

Satan is nothing in His hand. It is easier for God to crush Satan under our feet, than for you to crush a fly. God is infinitely stronger than Satan. Satan can no more hinder God from carrying us to glory than a little fly can, which you crush with your foot. 'He shall bruise Satan under your feet shortly.' Submit yourselves to God. Resist the devil, and he will flee from you.

An abundant entrance

He that soweth to his flesh shall of the flesh reap corruption;
but he that soweth to the Spirit shall of the
Spirit reap life everlasting.
Galatians 6 v 8

The whole Bible shows that Christians will be rewarded in eternity just in proportion to the way they have made use of their talents. Now, money is one talent. If you use it right, you will in no wise lose your reward. They that have done much for Christ shall have an abundant entrance; they that have done little shall have little reward.

The Saviour's desire

Father, I will that they also, whom thou hast given me,
be with me where I am;
John 17 v 24

He does not mean that we should be presently taken out of this world. Some of you that have come to Christ may, this day, be favoured with so much of the joy of heaven, and such a dread of going back to betray Christ in the world, that you may be wishing that this house were indeed the gate of heaven; you may desire that you might be translated from the table below at once to the table above. 'I am in a strait betwixt two, having a desire to depart and be with Christ.' Still Christ does not wish that. 'O pray not that thou shouldest take them out of the world, but that thou shouldst keep them from the evil.' 'Whither I go, thou canst not follow me now.' (like that woman in Brainerd's Journal - 'O blessed Lord, do come! Oh, do take me away! Do let me die and go to Jesus Christ. I am afraid, if I live, I shall sin again.'). He means, that when our journey is done, we should come to be with Him. Every one that comes to Christ has a journey to perform in this world. Some have a long, and some a short one. It is through a wilderness. Still Christ prays that at the end you may be with Him. Everyone that comes to Christ hath his twelve hours to fill up for Christ. 'I must work the works of him that sent me, while it is day.' But when that is done, Christ prays that you may be with Him. He means that you shall come to His Father's house with Him. 'In my Father's house are many mansions.' You shall dwell in the same house with Christ. You are never very intimate with a person till you see them in their own house, till you know them at home. This is what Christ wants with us - that we shall come to be with Him, at His own home. He wants us to come to the same Father's bosom with Him. 'I ascend to my Father and your Father.' He wants us to be in the same smile with Him, to sit on the same throne with Him, to swim in the same ocean of love with Him.

Robert Murray McCheyne's Manse, Dundee.

August

> "
>
> *He was one of the most complete ministers I ever met. He was a great preacher, an excellent visitor, a full orbed saint.*
>
> "

WILLIAM BLAIKIE

The wonderful grace of Christ

Not by works of righteousness which we have done, but
according to his mercy he saved us.
Titus 3 v 5

When the Holy Spirit leads a man to the cross, his heart there breaks from seeking salvation by his own righteousness. All his burden of performance and contrivances drops. First, the work of Christ appears so perfect, - the wisdom of God and the power of God - divine righteousness. 'I wonder that I should ever think of any other way of salvation. If I could have been saved by my own duties, my whole soul would now have refused it. I wonder that all the world did not see and comply with this way of salvation by the righteousness of Christ.' (Brainerd) Second, the grace of Christ appears so wonderful. That all this righteousness should be free to such a sinner! That I so long neglected, despised, hated it, put mountains between, and yet that He has come over the mountains! 'That thou mayest remember and be confounded, and never open thy mouth any more because of thy shame, when I am pacified toward thee for all that thou hast done'(Ezekiel 16 v. 63). Have you this broken heart - broken within sight of the cross? It is not a look into your own heart, or the heart of hell, but into the heart of Christ, that breaks the heart. Oh, pray for this broken heart! Boasting is excluded. To Him be glory. Worthy is the Lamb! All the struggles of a self-righteous soul are to put the crown on your own head instead of at the feet of Jesus.

They are not lost

... weeping may endure for a night, but joy cometh in the morning.
Psalm 30 v 5

This world is the vale of tears. There are always some mourning. No sooner is the tear dried on one cheek than it trickles down another. No sooner does one widow lay aside her weeds, that another takes them up. Those that are in Christ should weep as though they wept not; 'for the time is short'. Do you weep over those that died in the Lord? It is right to weep: 'Jesus wept'. Yet weep as though you wept not; 'for the time is short.' They are not lost, but gone before. The sun, when it sets, is not lost; it is gone to shine in another hemisphere; and so have they gone to shine in a brighter world. It is self-love that makes you mourn for them; for they are happy. You would not mourn if they were with a distant friend on earth - why do you mourn that they are with the sinner's Friend? 'They shall hunger no more, neither thirst any more, neither shall the sun light on them, nor any heat; for the Lamb, which is in the midst of the throne shall feed them, and shall lead them unto living fountains of waters: and God shall wipe away all tears from their eyes' (Revelation 7 vs. 16 - 17). 'The time is short'; and you will follow after. A few days, and you may be leaning together on the bosom of Jesus; you are nearer them today than you were yesterday. 'The time is short'; and you will meet with all the redeemed at the right hand of Christ. We shall mingle our voices in the new song, and wave together the eternal palm! 'Weep as though you wept not.'

August *third*

Cry for the wind

Awake, O north wind; and come thou south; blow upon my garden,
that the spices thereof may flow out.
Song of Solomon 4 v 16

These spices do not naturally grow in gardens. Even in the East there never was such a display as this. So the fragrant graces of the Spirit are not natural to the heart. They are brought from a far country. They must be carefully watched. They need the stream and the gentle zephyr. Oh, I fear most of you should hang your heads when Christ begins to speak of fragrant spices in your heart! Where are they? Are there not talkative, forward Christians? Are there not self seeking Christians? Are there not proud praying Christians? Are there not idle, bad working Christians? Lord, where are the spices. Verily, Christ is a bundle of myrrh. Oh to be like Him! Oh that every flower and fruit would grow! They must come from above. Many there are of whom one is forced to say, 'Well, they may be Christians; but I would not like to be next to them in heaven!' Cry for the wind!

August *fourth*

Forewarned is fore-armed

Confirming the souls of the disciples, and exhorting them to continue in the faith, and that we must through much tribulation enter into the kingdom of God.
Acts 14 v 22

We naturally shrink from pain. Many would like to go round; no, we must go through. Many would be willing to have a little; but no, we must through much tribulation enter the kingdom. There are three streams of trouble peculiar to believers.

Persecution - Let us go without the camp bearing His reproach - take up our cross daily. This is what Moses had to bear, and Lot, and all God's children, - trials of cruel mocking and scourging.

Temptations - There is a 'need be' for this also. Satan is a fearful enemy. Before conversion, we know little of him. Those who are determined to win glory, will feel his fiery darts. There is a design on Satan's part. He will not suffer us to go quietly into the kingdom. And on God's part, too, He wants us to know what we are saved from.

Concern for unconverted souls. - This is one of the deep afflictions of a child of God. He is afflicted for unconverted kindred. It may be father, mother, sister, brother, friend; the wife of his bosom, or the children of his love; unconverted neighbours, an unbelieving world. This is a sorrow he must carry with him to the grave.

O dear friends, make up your minds to carry the cross daily. Forewarned is to be fore-armed. All God's children go through these tribulations.

August *fifth*

God's delight

Likewise, I say unto you, there is joy in the presence of the angels of God over one sinner that repenteth.
Luke 15 v 10

When a hell-deserving sinner is enlightened in the knowledge of Christ - when he believes the record that God hath given concerning his Son, and joyfully consents that the Lord Jesus should be his surety, then the blood of Christ is as it were, sprinkled over that soul. When Aaron and his Sons were set apart for the priesthood, the blood of the ram was put upon the tip of their right ear, and the thumb of their right hand, and the great toe of their right foot, to signify that they were dipped in blood from head to foot; so when God looks upon a soul in Christ, He sees it dipped in the blood of the Saviour. He looks upon that soul as having suffered all that Christ suffered; therefore He delights in it.

His sense of justice is pleased. God has an infinite sense of justice His eyes behold the things that are equal. Now when He sees the blood of His Son sprinkled upon any soul, He sees that justice has had its full satisfaction in that soul, that that man's sins have been more fully punished than if he had borne them himself eternally.

His sense of mercy is pleased. He delighteth in mercy. Even when justice was crying out, 'Thou shalt surely slay the wicked,' His mercy was yearning over sinners, and He provided a ransom. And now when the sinner has laid hold on the ransom, mercy is poured down in forgiveness. God delighteth in mercy; He delights to forgive. It is sweet to notice how Jesus loves to forgive sins. In the story of the woman that washed His feet, how He seems to dwell on it! 'Her sins, which are many are forgiven.' And again He said unto her: 'Thy sins are forgiven thee.' And again, a third time: 'Go in peace.' And so God loves to forgive: 'There is joy in heaven over one sinner that repenteth.'

August *sixth*

Confidence in God
Nay, in all these things we are more than conquerors through him that loved us.
Romans 8 v 37

The world often comes against us like armed men; but, if God be for us, who can be against us'. 'The people shall be like bread.' It is as easy to overcome all opposition when God is with us, as for a hungry man to eat bread. It was God that girded Cyrus, though he did not know him. So he does still: worldly men are a rod in God's hand. God puts it this way or that way, to fulfil all His pleasure; and when He has done with it, He will break it in pieces, and cast it into the fire. 'So fear not them that kill the body, and after that, have no more that they can do.' Oh! if you would live by faith, you might live a happy life!

August *seventh*

Patient submission

**Submit yourselves therefore to God, Resist the devil,
and he will flee from you.**
James 4 v 7

Resignation is a very sweet grace: it can only be cultivated here. The believer has two kinds of graces - he has purity and resignation; God has purity, but God can have no resignation, for He has all sovereignty, He is almighty. Yet resignation to God's will is a very sweet grace; it is a flower that grows on the earth - it will not bloom yonder. It is much easier to go about a whole lifetime preaching, to preach night and day, than to be patient under sickness. There are many saints who suffered much upon earth, now shining the brightest in glory; just because they glorified God more than others by their patient submission.

August *eighth*

The pilgrim's staff

**Let your conversation be withour covetousness; and be content
with such things as ye have: for he hath said, I will never leave
thee, nor forsake thee.**
Hebrews 13 v 5

There is no time when you may be more inclined to think God has forsaken you, than when sin and Satan are raging. There is a difference from sin raging and sin reigning, though the soul may not see it. In such a time remember these words - 'I will never leave thee, nor forsake thee.' In a time of temptation, the believer should remember this promise. Jacob rested on it; Solomon rested on it: yea, it is a staff which has been leaned on by many believers, and you may lean on it too.

Prize the Word

Now ye are clean through the word which I have spoken unto you.
John 15 v 3

I believe He would sanctify without the Word, as He created angels and Adam holy, and as He sanctifies infants whose ear was never opened; but I believe in grown men He never will, but through the Word. When Jesus makes holy, it is by writing the Word in the heart: 'Sanctify them through thy truth.' When a mother nurses her child, she not only bears it in her arms, but holds it to her breast, and feeds it with the milk of her own breast; so does the Lord, He not only holds the soul, but feeds it with the milk of the Word. The words of the Bible are just the breathings of God's heart. He fills the heart with these, to make us like God. When you go much with a companion, and hear his words, you are gradually changed by them into his likeness; so when you go with Christ ,and hear his words, you are sanctified. Oh, there are some whom I could tell to be Christ's, by their breathing the same sweet breath! Those of you that do not read your Bible cannot turn like God - you cannot be saved. You are unsaveable; you may turn like the devil, but you never will turn like God. Oh, believers, prize the Word!

The divine Saviour

He was in the world, and the world was made by him,
and the world knew him not.
John 1 v 10

He was the Creator of all worlds: 'Without him was not anything made.' He was the Preserver of all worlds: 'By him all things consist', and hang together. All worlds, therefore, were His domain - He was Lord of all. He could say: 'Every beast of the forest is mine, and the cattle upon a thousand hills. I know all the fowls of the mountains: and the wild beasts of the field are mine. If I were hungry, I would not tell thee: for the world is mine, and the fullness thereof' (Psalm 50 vs. 10 - 12). All lands sang aloud to Him: the sea roared His praise, the cedars bowed before Him in lowly adoration. Nay, He could say: 'All things that the Father hath are mine' (John 16 v. 15); and He could speak to His Father of the glory which He had with Him before the world was. Whatever of power, glory, riches, blessedness, the Father had, dwelt with equal fullness in the Son; for He was in the form of God, and thought it no robbery to be equal with God. This was the riches of the Lord Jesus.

Oh, brethren! can you trust your salvation to such an one? You heard it was He that undertook to be the surety of sinners, and died for them. Can you trust your soul in the hands of such an one. Ah! surely if so rich and glorious a being undertake for us, He will not fail nor be discouraged, 'till he have set judgement in the earth; and the isles shall wait for his law'.

August *eleventh*

The sanctification of the saint

But of him are ye in Christ Jesus, who of God is made unto us wisdom, and righteousness, and sanctification, and redemption:
I Corinthians 1 v 30

Everyone whom Christ reconciles He makes holy, and confesses before His Father: 'Whom he justified, them he glorified'. If Christ has truly begun a good work in you, He will perform it to the day of Christ Jesus. Christ says: 'I am Alpha and Omega, the beginning and the ending.' Whenever He begins, He will make an end. Whenever He builds a stone on the foundation, He will preserve it unshaken to the end. Only make sure that you are upon the foundation - that you are reconciled - that you have true peace with God, and then you may look across the mountains and rivers that are between now and that day, and say: 'He is able to keep me from falling.' You have but two shallow brooks to pass through - sickness and death; and He has promised to meet you, and go with you, foot for foot. A few more tears - a few more temptations - a few more agonising prayers - a few more sacraments, and you will stand with the Lamb upon Mount Zion!

The unbelieving believer

And after eight days again his disciples were within, and Thomas
with them: then came Jesus, the doors being shut, and stood in the
midst, and said, Peace be unto you. Then saith he to Thomas, Reach
hither thy finger, and behold my hands; and reach hither thy hand,
and thrust it into my side: and be not faithless, but believing.
John 20 vs 26 - 28

When Thomas came to the meeting of disciples that evening, I doubt not his heart was very desolate. Unbelief and unhappiness always go together. An unbelieving believer is of all men most miserable. His brethren around him were full of joy, for they had seen the Lord. Mary still remembered the blessed tone of His voice when He said: 'Mary!' and she answered, 'Rabboni?' Peter was wondering over His amazing love when He said: 'Go tell the disciples, and Peter.' And the bosom of John was filled with a silent feeling of unutterable love. All were glad but one. That one was Thomas. But now, when Christ came in, when He revealed Himself a crucified but risen Redeemer, when He showed His special kindness to Thomas, the heart of Thomas could stand out no longer, and he cried out, in words of appropriating faith, before all: 'My Lord, and my God.'

See the end

Jesus answered and said unto him, What I do thou knowest
not now; but thou shalt know hereafter.
John 13 v 7

Perhaps you will say that they are an afflicted people. Some in poverty, some bereaved, some groaning on sick-beds. True, God dealeth with them as with sons. Often they cry 'These things are against me'. But really all is for them. If we could see the end as God does, we would see that every event is for the believer. When we get to the haven, we will see that every wind was wafting us to glory.

August *fourteenth*

A new creature

He that hath my commandments, and keepeth them, he it is that
loveth me: and he that loveth me shall be loved of my Father, and I
will love him, and will manifest myself to him.
John 14 v 21

Y ou are greatly mistaken if you think that to be a Christian is merely to have certain views and convictions and spiritual delights. This is all well; but if it leads not to a devoted life, I fear it is a delusion. 'If any man be in Christ, he is a new creature.'

August *fifteenth*

Here in is love!

But the Lord said unto Samuel, look not on his countenance, or on
the height of his stature; because I have refused him: for the Lord
seeth not as man seeth; for man looketh on the outward appearance,
but the Lord looketh on the heart.
I Samuel 16 v 7

H e was the only one that knew the wickedness of the beings for whom He died. He that searches the hearts of sinners died for them. His eye alone had searched their hearts; ay, was searching at the time He came. He knew what was in men; yet He did not abhor them on that account - He died for them. It was not for any goodness in man that He died for man. He saw none. It was not that He saw little sin in the heart of man. He is the only being in the universe that saw all the sin that is in the unfathomable heart of man. He saw to the bottom of the volcano - and yet He came and died for man. Herein is love! When publicans and sinners came to Him on earth, He knew what was in their hearts. His eye had rested on their bosoms all their life. He had seen all the lusts and passions that had ever rankled there. Yet in no wise did He cast them out. So with you. His eye hath seen all your sins - the vilest, darkest, blackest hours you have lived, His pure eye was resting on you. Yet he died for such , and invites you to come to Him, and will in no wise cast you out.

Temporal judgements

For the time is come that judgement must begin at the house of God:
and if it first begin at us, what shall the end be of them that obey not
the gospel of God?
I Peter 4 v 17

There are some sins which God visits with temporal judgements, as weakness of body, sickness, and death. When Ananias and Sapphira lied to the Holy Ghost, they fell down dead at the apostles' feet. When Herod gave not God the glory, he was eaten up of worms, and died upon his throne. So it is especially in profaning the Lord's table. This is God's word, who knows best: 'For this cause many are weak and sickly among you, and many sleep.'

My Beloved is mine

My beloved is mine, and I am his: he feedeth among the lilies.
Song of Solomon 2 v 16

If any man ask, 'How darest thou, sinful man, to call that divine Saviour thine?' the answer is here, 'For I am His.' He chose me from all eternity, wlse I never would have chosen Him. He sought after me, else I never would have sought after Him. He hath loved me, therefore I love Him. He hath chosen me, therefore I evermore choose Him. 'My beloved is mine.'

O worship the King

Praise ye the Lord. Praise the Lord, O my soul.
Psalms 146 v 1

Believers should praise God for what He is in Himself. Those that have never seen the Lord cannot praise Him. Those that have not come to Christ, have never seen the King in His beauty. An unconverted man sees no loveliness in God. He sees a beauty in the blue sky, in the glorious sun, in the green earth, in the spangling stars, in the lily of the field; but he sees no beauty in God. He hath not seen in Him, neither known Him; therefore there is no melody of praise in that heart.

When a sinner is brought to Christ, he is brought to the Father. Jesus gave himself for us, 'that he might bring us to God.' O! what a sight breaks in upon the soul - the infinite, eternal, unchangeable God! I know that some of you have been brought to see this sight.

August *nineteenth*

Love beyond compare

Let him kiss me with the kisses of his mouth:
for thy love is better than wine.
Song of Solomon 1 v 2

There is no love in this world like a mother's love. It is free, unbought, unselfish love. However much pain she has suffered on her child's account, however many troubles she has to bear for it, by night and by day, while it hangs upon her breast, still it is more precious than gold. There is something in her heart that clings to her weak, sickly, nay, even to her retarded boy. God's love to a soul in Christ is stronger than this love. The Psalmist compares it to a father's: 'Like as a father pitieth his children, so the Lord pitieth them that fear him.' And Malachi 3 v. 17: 'I will spare them, as a man spareth his own son that serveth him.' Again, Isaiah 66 v. 13: 'As one whom his other comforteth, so will I comfort you.'

August *twentieth*

Inseparable Christ

But one thing is needful: and Mary hath chosen that good part,
which shall not be taken away from her.
Luke 10 v 42

Mary hath chosen that good part, which shall not be taken away from her. Everything else can be taken away from you, your money, your friends, etc.: but if you have once embraced the Lamb of God, you have that good part which shall never be taken away from you. You are chosen to 'an inheritance incorruptible, undefiled, and that fadeth not away.' Then we can say without any fear, 'The lines are fallen unto me in pleasant places; yea, I have a goodly heritage.'

August *twenty-first*

Death of Stephen

And they stoned Stephen, calling upon God, and saying,
Lord Jesus, receive my spirit.
Acts 7 v 59

Stephen was the first to die as a martyr in the cause of Christ; and he seems to have resembled the Saviour more than any that followed after. His very face appeared like the face of an angel. His irresistible wisdom in arguing with the Jews was very like Christ. His praying for his enemies with his dying breath nearly in the same words as the Saviour, and his recommending his soul into the hands of the Lord Jesus, were in the same spirit of confidence as that in which Christ said: 'Father, into Thy hands I commend my spirit.' There cannot be a doubt that it was by looking unto Jesus that he became thus Christ-like. And the last view which he got of Christ seems especially to have given him that heavenly composure in dying which is so much above nature.

Two things are to be noticed: (1) that it was a sight of Christ at the right hand of God;

(2) that it was a sight of Christ standing there. Christ being at the right hand of God is mentioned sixteen times in the Bible; thirteen times He is described as seated there, twice as being there; but here only is He spoken of as standing. This appears to have made a deep and lively impression on the mind of Stephen, for he cries out: 'Behold, I see the heavens opened, and the Son of Man standing on the right hand of God'; and then, with a sweet assurance that Christ's hands were stretched out to receive him, he cried: 'Lord Jesus, receive my spirit.'

August *twenty-second*

When a believer falls

But I keep under my body, and bring it into subjection: lest that
by any means, when I have preached to others,
I myself should be a castaway.
I Corinthians 9 v 27

As long as a believer walks humbly with his God, his soul is at peace. The candle of the Lord shines on his head. He walks in the light as God walks in the light, and the blood of Jesus Christ his Son cleanseth him from all sin. But the moment that unbelief creeps in, he is led away into sin - like David, he falls very low. A believer generally falls lower than the world; and now he falls into darkness.

When Adam fell, he was afraid; and he hid himself from God among the trees of the garden, and made a covering of leaves. Alas! when a believer falls, he is also afraid - he hides from God. Now he has lost a good conscience, he fears to meet with God; he does not love the house of prayer; his heart is filled with suspicions. He says to himself: 'If I had been a child of God, would God have given me up to my own heart's lusts?' He refuses to return. 'There is no hope: no; for I have loved strangers, and after them will I go.' Though God has never been a wilderness or a land of darkness to the soul, yet he says: 'We are lords; we will come no more unto thee.' 'The Lord hath forsaken me, and my God hath forgotten me.' Ah! this is the bitterest of all kinds of desertion. If you put away faith and a good conscience, you will make shipwreck.

August *twenty-third*

Transformed

And Noah went in, and his sons, and his wife, and his sons' wives
with him, into the ark, because of the waters of the flood. Of clean
beasts, and of beasts that are not clean, and of fowls, and of every
thing that creepeth upon the earth.
Genesis 7 vs 7-8

All the beasts entered in. There came a lion and a lioness - they, too, entered in. And then there came in the tall cattle; there came a camel-lopard, with its long majestic neck bent down - it, too, entered in. And then came the birds; the eagle that loves to soar aloft in the sky, and feed upon its prey - it, too, entered in. And then the creeping things; there came a serpent, and perhaps, Noah might say when he saw them creeping along the ground, 'These will bite us' - but they, too, entered in. So, brethren, it is true that all kinds of sinners may enter in. And it is sweet to see what a change came over them when they entered in. The lion lay down beside the lamb, and the leopard beside the kid. So it is with those that came to Christ. The lion-like nature is changed into the gentle nature of the lamb - the proud man is made humble. 'If any man be in Christ Jesus he is a new creature: old things are passed away; behold, all things are become new.'

August *twenty-fourth*

The believer's prayer for divine teaching

Open thou mine eyes, that I may behold
wondrous things out of thy law.
Psalm 119 v 18

The law of God here spoken of is the Bible. In the days of David, the Law, or the Five Books of Moses, formed the greater part of the Bible, and so the whole was often called the Law. So, in the first verse, 'His delight is in the law of the Lord.' At verse 97 he says, 'O how love I thy law! it is my meditation all the day.' And here, 'Open thou mine eyes.'

The wondrous things seem to be the great things of an eternal world. David had looked on the wonders of this world - he had turned his enquiring eyes upon the wonders of nature, sun, moon, and stars, mountains, trees, and rivers. He had seen many of the wonders of art; but now, he wanted to see the spiritual wonders contained in the Bible. He wanted to know about God Himself in all His majesty, purity, and grace. He wanted to learn the way of salvation by a crucified Redeemer, and the glory that is to follow. These were the wondrous things David wanted to see.

'Open mine eyes.' - David was not blind - his eye was not dim. He could read the Bible from end to end, and yet he felt that he needed more light. He felt that he needed to see deeper, to have eyes of his understanding opened. He felt that if he had nothing but his own eyes and natural understanding, he would not discover the wonders which he panted to see. He wanted Divine teaching - the eye salve of the spirit; and therefore he would not open the Bible without this prayer, 'Open Thou mine eyes.

August *twenty-fifth*

Satan's objections answered

And the Lord said unto Satan, The Lord rebuke thee, O Satan; even
the Lord that hath chosen Jerusalem rebuke thee: is not this a brand
plucked out of the fire?
Zechariah 3 v 2

If any man sin we have an advocate with the Father, Jesus Christ the righteous. Christ is the advocate of every one He saves, and not only is He an advocate after conversion, but before, and throughout conversion. He answers Satan's objections. There are two arguments here by which He answers Satan. The first is the free election of God. Jerusalem was the chief city in the world for wickedness. They had sinned against light, against love, against long-suffering mercy. Yet Christ chose it. He might say, Grant that it is the chief of wickedness, yet God hath chosen it. Grant that that soul is the chief of sinners, yet the Lord is sovereign. 'I will have mercy on whom I will have mercy, and I will have compassion on whom I will have compassion.' This is the argument of Christ. Is it not strange that the very argument which troubles souls is the one which Christ uses as the reason why you should be saved? Let Satan say, you have sinned against light, against conviction, against love. Still, 'the Lord that hath chosen Jerusalem rebuke thee; is not this a brand plucked out of the fire?' This shuts Satan's mouth - this is an argument which he cannot answer. The second argument Christ employs is, the brand is already plucked out of the fire. Christ here says, whatever that sinner may have been, he is now plucked out of the fire. And thus all Satan's arguments are urged in vain.

August *twenty-sixth*

A lie of Satan

Wherefore let him that thinketh he standeth take heed lest he fall.
I Corinthians 10 v 12

I am tempted to think that I am now an established Christian - that I have overcome this or that lust so long, that I have got into the habit of the opposite grace - so that there is no fear. I may venture very near the temptation - nearer than other men. This is the lie of Satan. I might as well speak of gunpowder getting by habit a power of resisting fire, so as not to catch the spark. As long as powder is wet it resists the spark; but when it becomes dry it is ready to explode at the first touch. As long as the Spirit dwells in my heart He deadens me to sin, so that, if lawfully called through temptation, I may reckon upon God carrying me through. But when the Spirit leaves me I am like dry gunpowder. O for a sense of this!

A vessel unto honour

If a man therefore purge himself from these, he shall be a vessel unto honour, sanctified, and meet for the master's use, and prepared unto every good work.
II Timothy 2 v 21

I often pray, Lord, make me as holy as a pardoned sinner can be made.

Sin confessed and cleaned

If we confess our sins, he is faithful and just to forgive us our sins, and to cleanse us from all unrighteousness.
I John 1 v 9

I am persuaded that I ought to confess my sins more. I think I ought to confess sin the moment I see it to be sin; whether I am in company, or in study, or even preaching, the soul ought to cast a glance of abhorrence at the sin. If I go on with the duty, leaving the sin unconfessed, I go on with a burdened conscience, and add sin to sin. I think I ought at certain times of the day - my best times - say, after breakfast and after tea - to confess solemnly the sins of the previous hours, and to seek their complete remission.

August *twenty-ninth*
Complete holiness
For God hath not called us unto uncleanness, but unto holiness.
I Thessalonians 4 v 7

If you have truly joined yourself to Christ, you will never aim at less than complete holiness. It is told of a true child of God, that, in his agonising struggles after holiness, he would often lie upon the ground and cry, 'Lord, give me up to sickness, give me up to suffering, give me up to death, but give me not up to any sin.' If you have indeed joined yourself to Christ, you will have the same desire after universal holiness. 'Let not any iniquity have dominion over me.' 'Quicken Thou me in Thy way.'

August *thirtieth*
Lovest thou me more than these
So when they had dined, Jesus saith to Simon Peter, Simon, son of Jonas, lovest thou me more than these? He saith unto him, Yes, Lord; thou knowest that I love thee. He saith unto him, Feed my lambs.
John 21 v 15

Take heed what you love. Love what Jesus loved. Love not the world. Set your affection on things above, not on things on the earth. Love not money; it is the root of all evil. Love Jesus. Forgiven much, love much. Love God; He is worthy of all the love. Love the brethren; make them the chosen friends of your soul.

August *thirty-first*
Sanctified understanding
Thou through thy commandments hast made me wiser than mine enemies: for they are ever with me.
Psalm 119 v 98

A sanctified understanding is worth all the godless wisdom of earth and of hell. What fools the wisest of natural men appear when they die. Remember that, if you be joined to Christ, you will recieve the 'spirit of power, and of love, and of a sound mind.'

September

> "
>
> *His sanctity, his prayerfulness, his love for the Word of God, his passion for souls, make him a prince in Israel.*
>
> "

DR. DINSDALE T. YOUNG

September *first*

Precious Bible

*He shall feed his flock like a shepherd: he shall gather the lambs
with his arm, and carry them in his bosom, and shall gently
lead those that are with young.*
Isaiah 40 v 11

I shall never forget the story of a little girl in Belfast, in Ireland. She was at a Sabbath School, and gained a Bible as a prize for her good conduct. It became to her a treasure indeed. She was fed out of it. Her parents were wicked. She often read to them, but they became worse and worse. This broke Eliza's heart. She took to her bed and never rose again. She desired to see her teacher. When he came he said, 'You are not without a companion, my dear child,' taking up her Bible. 'No,' she replied -

'Precious Bible! what a treasure
Does the Word of God afford!
All I want for life or pleasure,
Food and med'cine, shield and sword.
Let the world account me poor,
Having this I ask no more.'

She had scarcely repeated the lines when she hung back her head and died. Beloved children, this is the way Jesus feeds His flock. He is a tender, constant, Almighty Shepherd. If you become His flock, He will feed you all the way to glory.

September *second*

Prize for Lord's day

*This is the day which the Lord hath made;
we will rejoice and be glad in it.*
Psalm 118 v 24

Prize the Lord's Day. The more that others despise and trample on it, love you it all the more. The louder the storm of blasphemy howls around you, sit the closer at the feet of Jesus. 'He must reign till He has put all enemies under His feet.' Diligently improve all holy time. It should be the busiest day of the seven; but only in the business of eternity. Avoid sin on that holy day. God's children should avoid sin every day, but most of all on the Lord's Day. It is a day of double cursing as well as of double blessing. The world will have to answer dreadfully for sins committed in holy time. Spend the Lord's Day in the Lord's presence. Spend it as a day in heaven. Spend much of it in praise and in works of mercy, as Jesus did.

The believer crowned

If we suffer, we shall also reign with him: if we deny him,
he also will deny us.
II Timothy 2 v 12

The late Duke of Hamilton had two sons. The eldest fell into consumption, when a boy, which ended in his death. Two ministers went to see him at the family seat, near Glasgow, where he lay. After prayer, the youth took his Bible from under his pillow, and turned up II Timothy 4 v. 7, 'I have fought a good fight, I have finished my course, I have kept the faith; henceforth, there is laid up for me a crown of righteousness;' and added, 'This, sirs, is all my comfort!' When his death approached, he called his younger brother to his bed, and spoke to him with great affection. He ended with these remarkable words, 'And now, Douglas, in a little time you will be Duke, but I shall be a King.'

Pictures

...because as he is, so are we in this world.
I John 4 v 17

If you love an absent person, you will love their picture. What is it that the sailor's wife keeps so closely wrapped in a napkin, laid up in her drawer among sweet smelling flowers? She takes it out morning and evening, and gazes at it through her tears. It is the picture of her absent husband. She loves it because it is like him. It has many imperfections, but still it is like him. Believers are the pictures of God in this world. The Spirit of Christ dwells in them. They walk as He walked. True, they are full of imperfections; still they are true copies. If you love Him, you will love them; you will make them your bosom friends.

September *fifth*

He will feed you

I am the door: by me if any man enter in, he shall be saved, and shall go in and out, and find pasture.
John 10 v 9

If Jesus has saved you He will feed you. he will feed your body. 'I have been young, and now am old, yet never saw I the righteous forsaken, nor his seed begging bread.'
The birds without barn or storehouse are fed,
From them let us learn to trust for our bread;
His saints what is fitting shall ne'er be denied,
So long as 'tis written - the Lord will provide.
He will feed your soul. He that feeds the little flower in the cleft of the craggy precipice, where no hand of man can reach it, will feed your soul with silent drops of heavenly dew.

September *sixth*

Peace perfect peace

And the very God of peace sanctify you wholly; and I pray God your whole spirit and soul and body be preserved blameless unto the coming of our Lord Jesus Christ.
I Thessalonians 5 v 23

God is to you the 'very God of peace'. Once He was to you the God of vengeance, but now he is the very God of peace. You can look back on a time when you lived under the wrath of the great God that made you. God was angry with you every day. You were altogether born in sin. Your heart was altogether depraved. You heaped up wrath against the day of wrath. Oh, do you not wonder that you are not in hell!

But you have fled to the bleeding Lamb, guilty and perishing. You have taken shelter in His wounds. You have this day openly accepted Him. Oh, if this be true, then God is the very God of peace to you. If I could this day go up into heaven, and open the books, and look into the records of the world, I would find your sins all blotted out, as a thick cloud; I would look up in the face of God and see Him smiling over you, saying, Thy sins and thine iniquities will I remember no more.

Dearly beloved and longed for, my joy and crown, rejoice evermore, for the God of vengeance is to you the very God of peace.

September *seventh*

Enough in Christ

Thou therefore, my son, be strong in the grace that is in Christ Jesus.
II Timothy 2 v 1

There is enough in Christ to supply the need of all His people. An old minister says, A child can carry little water from the sea in its two hands, and so it is little we get out of Christ. There are unsearchable riches in Him. Be strong in the grace that is in Him. Live out of yourself, and live upon Him; go and tell Him, that, since He requires all this of thee, He must give thee grace according to your need. My God shall supply all your need, according to His riches in glory by Christ Jesus. He hath showed you one that is good, even the fair Immanuel: now lean upon Him; get life from Him that shall never die; get living water from Him that shall never dry up. Let His hand hold you up amid the billows of this tempestuous sea. Let His shoulder carry you over the thorns of this wilderness. Look as much to Him for sanctification as for justification.

So will your walk be close with God,
Calm and serene your frame;
So purer light shall mark the road
That leads you to the Lamb.

September *eighth*

Our truest joy

And that ye put on the new man, which after God is created in righteousness and true holiness.
Ephesians 4 v 24

It is the chief glory and joy of a soul to be like God. You remember this was the glory of that condition in which Adam was created. 'Let us make man in our image, after our likeness.' His understanding was without a cloud. He saw, in some measure, as God seeth;

his will flowed in the same channel with God's will; his affections fastened on the same objects which God also loved. When man fell, we lost all this, and became children of the devil, and not children of God. But when a lost soul is brought to Christ, and receives the Holy Ghost, he puts off the old man, and puts on the new man, which after God is created in righteousness and true holiness. It is our true joy in this world to be like God. Too many rest in the joy of being forgiven, but our truest joy is to be like Him. Oh, rest not, beloved, till you are renewed after His image, till you partake of the divine nature. Long for the day when Christ shall appear, and we shall be fully like Him, for we shall see Him as He is.

September *ninth*

A Gospel of holiness

For the love of Christ constraineth us; because we thus judge, that if one died for all, then were all dead:
II Corinthians 5 v 14

The life of holiness is not what the world falsely represents it - a life of preciseness and painfulness, in which a man crosses every affection of his nature. There is no such thing as self-denial, in the popish sense of that word, in the religion of the Bible. The system of restrictions and self-crossings is the very system which Satan hath set up as a counterfeit of God's way of sanctifying. It is thus that Satan frightens away thousands from gospel peace and gospel holiness; as if to be a sanctified man were to be a man who crossed every desire of his being, who did everything that was disagreeable and uncomfortable to him. My friends, our text distinctly shows you that it is not so.

We are constrained to holiness by the love of Christ. The love of Him who loved us, is the only cord by which we are bound to the service of God. The scourge of our affection is the only scourge that drives us to duty. Sweet bands, and gentle scourges! Who would not be under their power?

Moses and Hobab

And Moses said unto Hobab, the son of Raguel the Midianite, Moses'
father in law, We are journeying unto the place of which the Lord
said, I will give it you: come thou with us, and we will do thee good:
for the Lord hath spoken good concerning Israel.
Numbers 10 v 29

So it was with Moses. Hobab had been his friend for forty years, in the land of Midian, where Moses married his sister, and lived in his father Raguel's house. In that time, I doubt not, Moses had told him much of Israel's God, and Israel's coming glory. Many a time, while they fed their flocks in this very wilderness, Moses had reasoned with him of righteousness, temperance and judgement to come, till Hobab trembled.

Still it would seem Hobab was not quite convinced. He doubted, he lingered. He had been awed by the terrors of Sinai, but not won by the love of Calvary. He did not know whether to go or stay. But the hour of decision came. He must decide now. Now was the heart of Moses stirred in him: 'Come thou with us, and we will do thee good; for the Lord hath spoken good concerning Israel.'

So it was with Paul, when he himself had tasted the joy and peace of believing; then says he: 'My heart's desire and prayer to God for Israel is, that they might be saved.'

So it was with Andrew: 'Andrew first findeth his own brother Simon, and saith unto him, We have found the Christ.'

So it was with the poor maniac whom Jesus healed: 'Go home, tell thy friends how great things the Lord hath done for thee, and how he hath had compassion on thee.'

So it was with the poor slave in Antigua, who used to pray that there might be a full heaven and an empty hell.

Question: Is it so with you? have you asked your friends to come with you? Have you a father whom you love? A mother that carried you at her breast? Have you a brother or sister? Are they lingering like Hobab? Oh! Will you not put in a word for Christ, and say: 'Come thou with us, and we will do thee good'? Have you a friend whom you love much, who knows nothing of Christ and of God, who is willing to die in the wilderness? Oh! Will you not win him to go with you to Israel's God and Israel's glory?

September *eleventh*

Faith is the victory

By faith the walls of Jericho fell down, after they were conpassed about seven days.
Hebrews 11 v 30

There is many a Jericho in our own heart walled up to heaven, many a fortress of sin, many giant lusts, which threaten our souls. 'O wretched man that I am, who shall deliver me from the body of this death?' 'If the Lord delight in us, he will bring us into the good land.' 'By faith the walls of Jericho fell down after they were compassed about seven days.' God made the walls of Jericho fall flat, by a mere breath of wind, a noise; so He is able still. Settle it in your hearts: there is no Jericho in your hearts

September *twelfth*

The believer's joy

Thou wilt shew me the path of life: in thy presence is fulness of joy; at thy right hand there are pleasures for evermore.
Psalm 16 v 11

The greatest joy of a believer in this world is to enjoy the presence of Christ - not seen, not felt, not heard, but still real - the real presence of the unseen Saviour. It is this that makes secret prayer sweet, and sermons sweet, and sacraments sweet, when we meet with Jesus in them: 'I have set the Lord always before me. Because he is at my right hand, I shall not be moved.'

Often Jesus hides His face, and we are troubled. We seek Him whom our soul loveth, but He is gone. We rise and seek, but find Him not. At the best, it is but half bliss to feel after an unseen Saviour. Suppose a husband and wife were parted by many seas. It is sweet to have letters and love tokens, and to see a friend who left him well; but this will not make up for his presence. So we mourn an absent Lord.

But when He comes we shall be with Him. 'In thy presence is fulness of joy; at thy right hand there are pleasures for evermore'. Here we have drops and gleams of pleasure. Christ could not be happy without us. We are His body. If one child of God were wanting, he would not be complete. We are His fulness. Hence His prayer: 'Father, I will that they also, whom thou hast given me, be with me where I am; that they may behold my glory, which thou hast given me' (John 17 v. 24)

We could not be happy without Christ. Take us to the golden pavement, the pearly gates, the songs, the thrones, the palms, the angels, we would still say, Where is the God-man that died for me? Where is the Angel that redeemed me from all evil? Where is Jesus? Where is the side that was pierced? 'We shall see his face.' The Lamb is the light thereof. We shall stand with the Lamb upon mount Zion. We shall never be parted more.

September *thirteenth*

Read the Bible

Open thou mine eyes, that I may behold
wondrous things ot of thy law.
Psalm 119 v 18

I f ye be led by the Spirit, ye will love the Bible. You will say, Oh, 'How love I Thy law, it is my meditation all the day.' Be determined to learn something new out of the Bible every day. 'I have lost a world of time,' said one, when dying. 'If I had another year to live, I would spend it in reading David's Psalms and Paul's Epistles.' Oh, be wiser in your Bibles than in the newspaper. What good will all that ever you read in the newspaper do when you are dying? Alas, for my beloved land, when the newspaper drives the Bible form its place by the cottage fire.

September *fourteenth*

A Covenant God

God is faithful, by whom ye were called unto the felowship
of his Son Jesus Christ our Lord.
I Corinthians 1 v 9

L ook around you. The world lying in wickedness is against you. 'I send you forth as sheep in the midst of wolves.' O, look down to hell; there are crafty devils - mighty spirits of evil, all, all against you. How then, should we hope such things from you? Ah! God is faithful, who also will do it. I lean my back upon the Rock of Ages, and

I feel there is enough in Him to enable me to stand against all the world. If you are joined to Christ, God is for you; God the Father is a shield all around you; God the Holy Ghost is within you. If you are joined to Christ, then God is a Covenant God to you.

September *fifteenth*

The third heaven of the believer's privileges

For none of us liveth to himself, and no man dieth to himself.
Romans 14 v 7

Surely this privilege is more than all that went before. Peace with God is a blessed thing, but it does not imply that the heart is burning with intense joy and love in view of a reconciled God. Access to His favour is a blessed thing; but it only implies liberty of coming before Him with acceptance. Joy in hope of glory is a blessed thing; but is in the very nature of it a happiness whose object is unenjoyed and afar off. Joy in tribulation, again, is a blessed thing; but it is a happiness which can only be enjoyed upon the earth. It is a joy, too, in spite of misery - a perfecting, but surely not a perfect joy. But joy in God is the most blessed thing of all. This is the third heaven of the believer's privileges - a joy which all the redeemed are sharing with angels - a joy begun in this world, made perfect in glory

September *sixteenth*

Because He lives

I am he that liveth, and was dead; and, behold,
I am alive for evermore, Amen;
Revelation 1 v 18

Believers, this is your Saviour. Soon you shall see Him as He is. Till then, 'Fear not.' Your Advocate is alive for evermore. He reigns for ever for His Church and people. All that divine wisdom is for us, His eyes are for us - His feet to tread down His and our enemies. He walks in the midst of the seven golden candlesticks, and holds the stars in His right hand.' There is no hiding of His glory now - no hiding of His power. He lives for us - no evil can befall us - 'Fear not.'

Much more

*If ye then, being evil, know how to give good gifts unto your children,
how much more shall your Father which is in heaven give
good things to them that ask him?*
Matthew 7 v 11

Men are apt to think that the only good of hiding in Christ is to save our souls, that when an awakened sinner hides in the Lord Jesus, he finds pardon of all sin and peace with God, but nothing more. But the whole Bible shows that there is much more in Christ; that when we hide in him, we are saved from all our distresses; from our troubles about health, about money, about the world. In Psalm 34, it is mentioned four times that when we come to Christ we are saved, not out of one trouble, but out of all our troubles: 'I sought the Lord; and he heard me, and delivered me from all my fears' 'This poor man cried, and the Lord heard him, and saved him out of all his troubles'. 'The righteous cry, and the Lord heareth, and delivereth them out of all their troubles.' 'Many are the afflictions of the righteous, yet the Lord delivereth him out of them all.' And the reason is plain. When we hide in Jesus, the God of providence becomes our God and Father, and we know He will make all things work together for our good. The Lord is our shepherd, we shall not want. Whatever temporal good may be taken away, we know that our eternal good is secure: 'I know whom I have believed, and am persuaded that he is able to keep that which I have committed unto him against that day.

Outlets of His glory

*But he was wounded for our transgressions, he was bruised for our
iniquities: the chastisement of our peace was upon him; and with his
stripes we are healed.*
Isaiah 53 v 5

The wounds of Christ were the greatest outlets of His glory that ever were. The divine glory shone more out of His wounds than out of all His life before. The veil was then rent in twain, and the full heart of God allowed to stream through. It was a human body that writhed, pale and racked, upon the accursed tree; they were human hands that were pierced so rudely by the nails; it was human flesh that bore that deadly gash upon the side; it was human blood that streamed from hands, and feet, and side; the eye that meekly turned to His Father was a human eye; the soul that yearned over His mother was a human soul. But oh, there was divine glory streaming through all! every wound was a mouth to speak of the grace and love of God!

September *nineteenth*

A *harp of praise*

How shall we sing the Lord's song in a strange land?
Psalm 137 v 4

Every believer has a harp. Every heart that has been made new is turned into a harp of praise. The mouth is filled with laughter, the tongue with divinest melody. Every true Christian loves praise; the holiest Christians love it most. But when the believer falls into sin and darkness, his harp is on the willows, and he cannot sing the Lord's song, for he is in a strange land.

September *twentieth*

Holiness

Having therefore these promises, dearly beloved, let us cleanse ourselves from all filthiness of the flesh and spirit, perfecting holiness in the fear of God.
II Corinthians 7 v 1

When a soul comes to close with Christ he is not made perfectly holy all at once: 'The path of the just is as the shining light, that shineth more and more unto the perfect day.' Just as you have seen the day struggling with the darkness, then with clouds, till the sun bursts forth in meridian splendour; so it is with the holiness of a Christian. Just as in the richest lands, after the deepest ploughing, weeds will still grow up among the corn; so, many roots of bitterness remain in the believer's heart.

Paul thanked God for the grace that was given to the Corinthians, that they came behind in no gift; and yet he says they had strife, and envy, and divisions, so that he could not call them spiritual, but carnal So is it with every Christian heart. Weeds grow up in the best cultivated gardens. There is enough in Christ to supply all our need It is our own fault that we are not holy as God is holy It is not in Christ, but in ourselves, that we are straitened. The shower of grace is plentiful enough, and more than enough; we do not open our mouths wide.

But every soul in Christ hates sin and pants after holiness. Nothing makes him pant more after God than corruption striving within. Paul never prayed more earnestly than when he had the thorn in his flesh. The thorn in the flesh makes us pant after God.

September *twenty-first*

Distance makes no difference

But I have prayed for thee, that thy faith fail not: and when thou art converted, strengthen thy brethren.
Luke 22 v 32

Brethren, if you had been behind some of the trees on Tabor's mount, and heard Him mention your name in prayer, saying, I do not pray for Peter only, or for James, or John, but for this soul. Father, sanctify this soul through thy truth. Father, I will that this soul be with me where I am, that it may behold my glory. Say, douting sinner, if you had heard Christ mentioning thy name, would it not have given you peace? Does distance make any difference? Suppose you heard a friend praying for you in the next room, or suppose you were told that a friend residing in a foreign land prayed for you, would it make any difference? Now, suppose you are told Christ prays for you - for He prays for all His believing people - will you not take the comfort of it?

September *twenty-second*

Fullness of joy

Your heart shall rejoice, and your joy no man taketh from you.
John 16 v 22

For my own part, I never knew what joy was till I felt that Jesus had died for me - that he lived for me and reigned for me. The world can give you little joy; but here is fullness of joy.

September *twenty-third*

Faith's view of Christ

And when he had so said, he showed unto them his hands and his
side. Then were the disciples glad when they saw the Lord.
John 20 v 20

When the Lord of glory left His Father's bosom, and came into this world, we are sure it was for a purpose suited to His divine nature. Christ came to make men glad. It was said of Him, 'The Spirit of the Lord God is upon me, because the Lord hath appointed me to preach good tidings unto the meek.' (Isaiah 61 v. 1.) Ah! sure, He must be a good Saviour that was to bind up broken hearts, and to make all men glad. Therefore, when He came, He said, 'That their joy might be full.' And you see in the verse before our text, His first words to His disciples were, 'Peace be unto you.' But the devil wants you to believe that we want to take away your mirth and joy. He is a liar, and he was a liar from the beginning. Jesus came not to destroy men's lives, but to save them; so do we. We come to break your false joy - to awaken you from your dream - before you be dashed into the burning lake. Ah! we come to give you fullness of joy that cannot wither - joy that cannot die. True, believers have sorrow; they have a poor frail body, and they may have false friends. They may have ungodly children; they have temptations and persecutions. The world knows nothing of these sorrows. But they have a joy that the world cannot give or take away. They have a joy to balance all their sorrows; they have 'joy unspeakable and full of glory'. It is a joy that will never die. it will be brighter and brighter throughout an endless eternity.

September *twenty-fourth*

Take away the stone

Jesus said, Take ye away the stone. Martha, the sister of him
that was dead, saith unto him, Lord, by this time he stinketh:
for he hath been dead four days.
John 11 v 39

Christ's ways are not as our ways, nor His thoughts like our thoughts. One would have thought that He would have commanded the stone to fly back by His own word.

When he rose from the dead Himself, 'the angel of the Lord descended from heaven, and came and rolled back the stone from the door and sat upon it'; but He did not do so now. He said to the men, 'Take ye away the stone' for two reasons. First, He wanted to bring out Martha's unbelief, that it might be made manifest. Unbelief in the heart is like evil humour in a wound - it festers; and therefore Jesus wanted to draw it out of Martha's heart. Second, to teach us to use the means. The men around the grave could not give life to dead Lazarus, but they could roll back the stone. Now Jesus was about to use His divine power in awaking the dead, but He would not take away the stone.

Have any of you an unconverted friend for whom you pray? You know it is only Christ that can five him life, it is only Christ that can call him forth. Yet you can roll away the stone - you can use the means, you can bring your friend under the faithful preaching of the gospel. Speak to him, write to him. 'Take away the stone.'

September *twenty-fifth*

The voice of the shepherd

And when he putteth forth his own sheep, he goeth before them,
and the sheep follow him: for they know his voice. And a stranger
will they not follow, but will flee from him: for they know
not the voice of strangers.
John 10 vs 4-5

You know, brethren, this is the characteristic of the sheep of the east, they know the shepherds voice. There was once a traveller in the east who denied that they knew the voice of the shepherd, and contended that it was the person they knew; and to prove it, they changed clothes. The person called the sheep, ånd they moved not; but when the shepherd called them, they instantly followed him. Now, this is just the way with Christ and His sheep. Christ may be disguised, but faith hears His voice. The first time they hear His voice is the time of conversion. You remember Zaccheus, he was up in the sycamore tree, and he might think, 'Christ's word will not reach me'; but Christ said to him. 'Come down, Zaccheus, for today I must abide at thy house.' The voice of the Shepherd reached him. This was the first day that Zaccheus heard the Shepherd's voice. You remember Lydia, she sat among the

Grecian matrons by the riverside, and heard Paul preach. Someone opened her heart, and said, 'Come away'; it was the voice of the Shepherd. 'The Lord opened the heart of Lydia to attend unto the things that were spoken.' It was the outward voice of Paul, but it was the inward voice of Christ.

September *twenty-sixth*

The wonder of it all

*Hearken unto me, O house of Jacob, and all the remnant of
the house of Israel, which are borne by me from the belly,
which are carried from the womb: And even to your old age I am he;
and even to hoar hairs will I carry you: I have made, and I will bear:
even I will carry and will deliver you.*
Isaiah 46 vs 3-4

There are times in the life of a believer when he is like a traveller who has arrived at some high eminence; he can look back on the way he has gone and the way he has yet to go. So this is a passage where God tells us what He has done and what He will yet do. The history of a believer is wonderful, whether we look backward or forward. If we look back, there is election in a past eternity; and if we look forward, there is deliverance and final victory. As Christ's name is 'Wonderful,' so all the members of His body are wonderful, for they are 'men wondered at.'

September *twenty-seventh*

Look to the cross

*Who gave himself for our sins, that he might deliver us from this
present evil world, according to the will of God and our Father.*
Galatians 1 v 4

Some are saying, Oh that the world were crucified to me, and I to the world! Oh that my heart were dead as a stone to the world, and alive to Jesus! Do you truly wish it? Look, then, to the cross. Behold the amazing gift of love. Salvation is promised to a look. Sit down, like Mary, and gaze upon a crucified Jesus. So will the world become a dim and dying thing. When you gaze upon the sun, it makes everything else dark; when you taste honey, it makes everything else tasteless: so when your soul feeds on Jesus it takes away the sweetness of all earthly things, - praise, pleasure, fleshly lusts, all lose their sweetness. Keep a continued gaze. Run, looking unto Jesus. Look, till the way of salvation by Jesus fills up the whole horizon, so glorious and peace-speaking. So will the world be crucified to you, and you unto the world.

September *twenty-eighth*

Love for the Lord's day

Upon the first day of the week let every one of you lay by
him in store, as God hath prospered him, that there be
no gatherings when I come.
I Corinthians 16 v 2

All days of the year are Christ's, but He hath marked out one in seven as peculiarly His own. 'He hath made it,' or marked it out. Just as He planted a garden in Eden, so He hath fenced about this day and made it His own.

This is the reason why we love it, and would keep it entire. We love everything that is Christ's. We love His word. It is better to us than thousands of gold and silver. 'O how we love His law! it is our study all the day.' We love His house. It is our trysting-place with Christ, where He meets with us and communes with us from off the mercy-seat. We love His table. It is His banqueting house, where His banner over us is love - where He looses our bonds,and anoints our eyes, and makes our hearts burn with holy joy. We love His people, because they are His, members of His body, washed in His blood, filled with His Spirit, our brothers and sisters for eternity. And we love the Lord's day, because it is His. Every hour of it is dear to us - sweeter than honey, more precious than gold. It is the day He rose for our justification. It reminds us of His love, and His finished work, and His rest. And we may boldly say that man does not love the Lord Jesus Christ who does not love the entire Lord's day.

September *twenty-ninth*

A holy carefulness

But all things that are reproved are made manifest by the light: for whatsoever doth make manifest is light.

Ephesians 5 v 13

Remember you must have a holy carefulness - 'Seek ye first the kingdom of God and his righteousness, and all these things shall be added unto you.' Dear brethren, some of you will say, How is it possible? Do not I live in an ungodly family? Do I not live in Sodom? But, dear brethren, here is the secret. If you will not be like the world, be transformed to it. God is able to keep you from falling and to present you faultless before the presence of His glory with exceeding joy. God is able to enlarge your heart so that you will run and not weary in God's ways. Then be of good courage, for there is enough in Christ to satisfy you. Do you want to be holy? Then God wishes to make you holy. Then God's will and yours are one. Say, then, 'Make me holy, I want to be holy.' Holiness is the brightest attribute of Jehovah. Ah! I fear we are not living up to what is in Christ, or we would not live as we do. How much useless talk and conversation is there? Oh! the time of our life is more than sufficient to have wrought the will of the flesh. Let us now live to Him. Let us give ourselves away to Christ - solemnly to Him; give your wills and affections to Him for time and for eternity. The grace of the Lord Jesus be with your spirit. Amen.

September *thirtieth*

A vent for His love

Therefore doth my Father love me, because I lay down my life, that I might take it again.

John 10 v 17

Therefore doth my Father love me because I lay down my life. I do not know any word in the Bible that is more sweet to meditate on than the love of the Father to the Son. There are many things that induce the Father to love the Son. He loved Him for His Godhead. But here is another reason why the Father loves the Son - He loves Him for His holy manhood. 'He was holy, harmless, undefiled, and separate from sinners.' God never saw anything so like Himself. When God made Adam, He said, 'It is very good'; but oh! when He saw Jesus, he saw a loveliness in Him such as He never saw in any created thing. But here is another reason why the Father loves Him - 'Therefore doth my Father love me, because I lay down my life.' We are told that He grew in favour both with God and man. He was every day fulfilling a part of His holy obedience, until He came to the last, and then the Father saw obedience as He had never seen before. Oh, brethren! it was love that was never seen before, that He should die for the lowest - for the vilest. And that appears to be another reason why Jesus died: it is, that the Father got a vent for his love to flow out to sinners - 'Therefore doth my father love me, because I lay down my life.'

Robert Murray McCheyne around 29 years of age.

October

> "
>
> *McCheyne's life tells us about a quality of Christian life and ministry that is sadly lacking in the Church today.*
>
> "
>
> JOHN J. MURRAY

October *first*

No thorn, no throne

And I said unto him, Sir, thou knowest. And he said to me, These are
they which came out of great tribulation, and have washed their
robes, and made them white in the blood of the Lamb.
Revelation 7 v 14

Every one that gets to the throne must put their foot upon the thorn. The way to the crown is by the cross. We must taste the gall if we are to taste the glory. When justified by faith, God led them into tribulations also. When God brought Israel through the Red Sea, He led them into the wilderness; so, when God saves a soul, He tries it. He never gives faith without trying it. The way to Zion is through the valley of Baca. You must go through the wilderness of Jordan if you are to come to the Land of Promise. Some believers are much surprised when they are called to suffer. They thought they would do some great thing for God; but all that God permits them to do is to suffer. Go round every one in glory, - every one has a different story, yet every one has a tale of suffering. One was persecuted in his family, - by his friends and companions; another was visited by sore pains and humbling disease. - neglected by the world; another was bereaved of children; another had all these afflictions meeting in one, - deep called unto deep. Mark! all are brought out of them. It was a dark cloud, but it passed away; the water was deep, but they have reached the other side. Not one of them blames God for the road He led them: 'Salvation' is their only cry. Is there any of you, dear children, murmuring at your lot? Do not sin against God. This is the way God leads all His redeemed ones. You must have a palm as well as a white robe. No pain, no palm; no cross, no crown; no thorn, no throne; no gall, no glory. Learn to glory in tribulations also. 'I reckon that the sufferings of this present time are not worthy to be compared with the glory that shall be revealed in us.'

October *second*

Make haste my beloved

Make haste, my beloved, and be thou like to a roe or to a young hart
upon the mountains of spices.
Song of Solomon 8 v 14

It is the presence of Christ that makes a sweet time of refreshing in a Church. When He comes leaping on the mountains, skipping upon the hills, the flowers immediately appear on the earth. The Lord's people are quickened in all their graces; they begin to sing songs of deliverance; anxious souls spring up like the grass, and the whole garden of the Lord sends out spices. Ah! if the Lord Jesus were to come in here with power, I would preach and you would hear in another way than we do. I could not be so hard-hearted, and you would be melted under His word. Oh! will you not pray, 'Make haste, my beloved, and be thou like to a roe, or to a young hart upon the mountains of spices.' Is not such a time desirable?

October *third*

A hymn of prayer

And Jabez was more honourable than his brethren: and his mother called his name Jabez, saying, Because I bare him with sorrow. And Jabez called on the God of Israel, saying, Oh that thou wouldest bless me indeed, and enlarge my coast, and that thine hand might be with me, and that thou wouldest keep me from evil, that it may not grieve me! And God granted him that which he requested.
I Chronicles 4 vs 9-10

O God of Israel, hear my prayer!
Let me thy richest blessings share;
Thy blessings shall my portion be;
Oh! let that blessing rest on me!

If shining suns my path attend,
And all their cheering influence lend;
Thy blessing still I'll most desire,
To that my highest hopes aspire.

Or, if affliction's storm shall low'r,
I'll trust thee in the darkest hour;
On thee I'll rest my anxious mind,
And in thy blessing comfort find.

'Preserve me from the snares of sin,
And ever keep my conscience clean:
Till all the cares of life shall cease,
And, blessing thee, I die in peace!'

Thus pious Jabez often prayed,
Reclining on Jehovah's aid;
And all who seek the Lord shall find
The God of Jabez still as kind.

O children! who assemble here,
With holy love and humble fear.
Like him present the fervent prayer,
And in God's richest blessing share.

October *fourth*

Family government

For I know him, that he will command his children and his
household after him, and they shall keep the way of the Lord,
to do justice and judgment; that the Lord may bring upon
Abraham that which he hath spoken of him.
Genesis 18 v 19

There are three things very remarkable in these words.

1. That Abraham used parental authority in governing his family: 'I know him, that he will command his children and servants after him.' He did not think it enough to pray for them, or to teach them, but he used the authority which God had given him. He commanded them.

2. That he cared for his servants as well as his children. In Genesis 14 v. 14, we learn that Abraham had 318 servants born in his house. He lived after the manner of patriarchal times, as the Arabs of the wilderness do to this day. His family was very large, and yet he did not say, 'They are none of mine.' He commanded his children and his household.

3. His success. 'They shall keep the way of the Lord.' It is often said that the children of good men turn out ill. Well, here is a good man, and a good man doing his duty by his children - and here is the result. His son Isaac was probably a child of God from his earliest years. There is every mark of it in his life. And what a delightful specimen of a believing, prayerful servant was Eliezer! (Genesis 24)

It is the duty of all believers to rule their houses well.

Jesus bids us shine

Let your light so shine before men, that they may see your good
works, and glorify your Father which is in heaven.
Matthew 5 v 16

Shine with Christ's light. The moon rises and shines, but not with her own light; she gathers all from the sun; so do you. Shine in such a way that Christ shall have all the glory. They shine brightest who feel most their own darkness, and are most clothed in Christ's brightness. Oh, wherever you go, make it manifest that your light and peace all come from Him; that it is by 'looking unto Jesus' that you shine, and that your holiness all comes from union with Him. Shine in your closet in secret prayer. Ah! let your face shine in secret communion with God. Shine in your family. Shine in your town; that, when you mingle with the crowd, it may be as if an angel shook his wings. Shine in the world. Oh! let your heart's desire and prayer be, that every soul may be saved. Be like Christ Himself, who is not willing that any should perish.

Care of new converts

He saith unto him, the third time, Simon, son of Jonas, lovest thou
me? Peter was grieved because he said unto him the third time,
Lovest thou me? And he said unto him, Lord, thou knowest all things;
thou knowest that I love thee. Jesus saith unto him, Feed my sheep.
John 21 v 17

Do not forget to carry on the work in hearts brought to a Savior. I feel this was one of my faults in the ministry. Nourish babes; comfort downcast believers; counsel those perplexed; perfect that which is lacking in their faith. Prepare them for some trials. I fear most christians are quite unready for days of darkness.

October *seventh*

A new name

To him the porter openeth; and the sheep hear his voice; and he
calleth his own sheep by name, and leadeth them out.
John 10 v 3

This first of all, shows the complete knowledge he has of the sheep. You remember Zaccheus, when he was a stray sheep, Christ said to him when he was in the tree, 'Come down; for today I must abide at thine house.' You remember Nathaniel, when a stray sheep under the fig-tree, 'he saw him.' You remember, after His resurrection, He saw Mary and said to her, 'Mary'; and she turned herself, and said unto Him, 'Rabboni: which is to say, Master.' So it is still. Ministers do not know you; elders do not know you; but Christ knows you, and He calls His own sheep by name, and they follow Him. And this implies, also, the love of Christ. You know when you love one, you love their name. Christ does not only know you, but He calls you by His name. He called Bethany, 'the town of Mary and her sister Martha.' Christ loves the names of those for whom He died. Your names are graven on His heart, and on the palms of His hands; and this shows He changes their names. He said to Abraham, 'Thy name shall no more be called Abram, but Abraham shall thy name be.' And you remember he said of Peter, 'Thy name shall be called Peter,' which means a stone. And it is said of the Jews, 'I have called thee by my name, thou art mine.' So it implies that they get a new name, that is, a new nature. And, when we come to the temple above, He says, 'Him that overcometh will I make a pillar in the temple of my God, and he shall go no more out; and I will write upon him the name of my God, and the name of the city of my God, which is new Jerusalem, which cometh down out of heaven from my God; and I will write upon him my new name.' And you that are of the world, if you will come, you will get a new name.

October *eighth*

Be found on the right side

Then Moses stood in the gate of the camp, and said,
Who is on the Lord' side? let him come unto me.
Exodus 32 v 26

There are three things which Christ does as a king to every saved soul. The first is at conversion, see Acts 5 v. 31: 'Him hath God exalted with his right hand to be a Prince and a Saviour, for to give repentance to Israel, and forgiveness of sins.' You will notice that the office of Christ as King is to give repentance and forgiveness of sins. It is His work to say, 'Love!' Ah! friends, has He done this to you? Observe, it is not the work of man: 'He will not give his glory to another, neither his praise to graven images.' It is from His throne at the right hand of God that he sends the Spirit, and makes three thousand cry out, 'Men and brethren, what shall we do to be saved?' It is a most affecting truth I have shewn you, that you may be a member of His kingdom. and not a member of His grace. Another kingly act of Christ over His Church is to forgive sins. 'The Son of man hath power on earth to forgive sins.' Ah! dear friends, it is a kingly act to give pardon. The third work that Christ does as a King over His body is to sanctify them. It is written in Micah, 'Who is a God like unto thee, that pardoneth iniquity, and passeth by the transgressions of the remnant of his heritage? he retaineth not his anger for ever, because he delighteth in mercy,' (Micah 7 v. 18). Those whom the king pardons he subdues. Ah! dear friends, enquire if Christ is your King, by his subduing you. How happy are those of you who can say, Christ is my King! Dear friends, enquire if you are under this third crown. The third is the sweetest of all. He wears all His other crowns for this one. It is interesting to notice that in the first ages of the Church, Christians were martyred for His prophetical office: and it is reserved, it may be, for us to be martyred for His kingly office: it was this, you remember the Covenanters were martyred for. How necessary then, to be found on the right side!

October *ninth*

All to Jesus I surrender

What could have been done more to my vineyard,
that I have not done in it?
Isaiah 5 v 4

He thought nothing too much to do and to suffer for us. While we were yet sinners, Christ died for us. Greater love than this hath no man. All His life, between the manger at Bethlehem and the cross of Calvary, was spent in labours and infinite sufferings for us. All that we needed to suffer, He suffered; all that we need to obey,

He obeyed. All His life in glory He spends for us. He ever liveth to make intercession for us. He is head over all things for us - makes every thing in all worlds work together for our good. It is all but incredible that each person of the Godhead has made Himself over to us to be ours. The Father says. 'I am thy God;' the Son, 'Fear not, for I have redeemed thee;' the Holy Ghost makes us a temple, 'I will dwell in them and walk in them.' Is it much that we should do all we can for Him - that we should give ourselves up to Him who gave Himself for us?

October *tenth*

It will be worth it all

Now he that planteth and he that watereth are one: and every man shall receive his own reward according to his own labour.
I Corinthians 3 v 8

The labour that Christ blesseth is believing labour. It is not words of human wisdom, but words of faith, that God makes arrows. The word of a little maid was blessed in the house of Naaman the Syrian. 'Follow me,' was made the arrow to pierce the heart of Matthew. It is all one to God to save, whether with many, or with them that have no might. If you would do all you can, the town would be filled with the fragrance. Christ will reward it. He defended Mary's work of love, and said it should be spoken of over all the world, and it will yet be told in the judgment. A cup of cold water He will not pass over. 'Well done good and faithful servant.'

October *eleventh*

The blessed prayer of the bride

He which testifieth these things saith, Surely I come quickly.
Amen. Even so, come, Lord Jesus.
Revelation 22 v 20

Even the most enlightened believers are walking here in a darksome night, or twilight at most; and the visits of Jesus to the soul do but serve to make the surrounding darkness more visible. But the night is far spent, the day is at hand. The day of eternity is breaking in the east. The Sun of Righteousness is hasting to rise upon our world, and the shadows are preparing to flee away. Till then, the heart of every true believer, that knows the preciousness of close communion with the Saviour, breathes the earnest prayer, that Jesus would often come again, thus sweetly and suddenly, to lighten him in his darksome pilgrimage. Ah, yes, my friends, let every one, who loves the Lord Jesus in sincerity, join now in the blessed prayer of the bride - 'Until the day break and the shadows flee away, turn, my beloved, and be thou like a roe or a young hart upon the mountains of Bether.'

October *twelfth*

A glorious garment

But the father said to his servants, Bring forth the best robe, and put
it on him; and put a ring on his hand, and shoes on his feet.
Luke 15 v 22

As long as you live in your mortal body, you will be faulty in yourself. It is a soul ruining error to believe anything else. O if ye would be wise, be often looking beneath the robe of the Redeemer's righteousness to see your own deformity. It will make you keep faster hold of His robe, and keep you washing in the fountain. Now, when Christ brings you before the throne of God, He will clothe you with His own fine linen, and present you faultless. O it is sweet to me to think how soon you shall be the righteousness of God in Him. What a glorious righteousness that can stand the light of God's face! Sometimes a garment appears white in dim light; when you bring it into sunshine you see the spots. O prize, then, this Divine righteousness, which is your covering.

October *thirteenth*

Faultness

Now unto him that is able to keep you from falling, and to present
you faultless before the presence of his glory with exceeding joy.
Jude v 24

My heart sometimes sickens when I think upon the defects of believers; when I think of one Christian being fond of company, another vain, another given to evil speaking. O aim to be holy Christians! - bright, shining Christians. The heaven is more adorned by the large bright constellations than by many insignificant stars; so God may be more glorified by one bright Christian than by many indifferent ones. Aim at being that one.

Soon we shall be faultless. He that begun will perform it. We shall be like Him, for we shall see Him as He is. When you lay down this body, you may say - farewell lust for ever - farewell my hateful pride - farewell hateful selfishness - farewell strife and envying - farewell being ashamed of Christ. O this makes death sweet indeed! O long to depart and to be with Christ!

October *fourteenth*

Hidden

O my dove, that art in the clefts of the rock, in the secret places of the stairs, let me see thy countenance, let me hear thy voice; for sweet is thy voice, and thy countenance is comely.
Song of Solomon 2 v 14

As a timorous dove pursued by the vulture, and well nigh made a prey, with fluttering anxious wing, hides itself deeper than ever in the clefts of the rock, and in the secret places of the precipice, so the backslidden believer, whom Satan has desired to have, that he might sift him as wheat, when he is restored once more to the all-gracious presence of his Lord, clings to Him with fluttering, anxious faith, and hides himself deeper than ever in the wounds of his Saviour. Thus it was that the fallen Peter, when he had so grievously denied his Lord, yet, when brought again within sight of the Saviour, standing upon the shore, was the only one of the disciples who girt his fisher's coat unto him, and cast himself into the sea to swim to Jesus; and just as that backslidden apostle, when again he had hidden himself in the clefts of the Rock of Ages, found that the love of Jesus was more tender towards him than ever, when he began that conversation, which, more than all the others in the Bible, combines the kindest of reproofs with the kindest of encouragements, 'Simon, son of Jonas, lovest thou me more than these?' just so does every backslidden believer find, that when again he is hidden in the freshly opened wounds of his Lord, the fountain of His love begins to flow afresh, and the stream of kindness and affection is fuller and more overflowing than ever, for His word is, 'Oh, my dove, that art in the clefts of the rock, in the secret places of the precipice, let me see thy countenance, let me hear thy voice; for sweet is thy voice, and thy countenance is comely.'

The broken heart

The sacrifices of God are a broken spirit: a broken and a contrite heart, O God, thou wilt not despise.
Psalm 51 v 17

No Psalm expresses more fully the experience of a penitent believing soul: - First, His humbling confession of sin, (vs. 3-5). Second, His intense desire for pardon through the blood of Christ, (v.7). Third, His longing after a clean heart, (v.10). Fourth, His desire to render something to God for all His benefits. 1. He says, I will teach transgressors thy ways. 2. My lips shall show forth thy praise. 3. He will give a broken heart, vs. 16, 17. Just as, long ago, they used to offer slain lambs in token of thanksgiving, so he says he will offer up to God a slain and broken heart. Every one of you, who has found the same forgiveness, should come to the same resolution - offer up to God this day a broken heart.

Reflect His image

He that shewed thee, O man, what is good; and what doth the Lord require of thee, but to do justly, and to love mercy, and to walk humbly with thy God?
Micah 6 v 8

God requires His redeemed ones to be holy. - If you are His brethren, He will have you righteous, holy men. First, He requires you to do justly - to be just in your dealings between man and man. This is one of His own glorious features. He is a just God. 'Shall not the Judge of all the earth do right?' 'He is my Rock, and there is no unrighteousness in Him.' Are you come to Him by Jesus? - He requires you to reflect His image. Are you His child? - you must be like Him. O brethren, be exact in your dealings. Be like your God. Take care of dishonesty; take care of trickery in business. Take care of crying up your goods when selling them, and crying them down when buying them. 'It is nought, it is nought, sayeth the buyer, but when he is gone his way, he boasteth.' It shall not be so among you. God requires you to do justly.

Secondly, He requires you to love mercy. - This is the brightest feature in the character of Christ. If you are in Christ, drink deep of His Spirit; God requires you to be merciful. The world is selfish, unmerciful. An unconverted mother has no mercy on the soul of her own child. She can see it dropping into hell without mercy. O the hellish cruelty of unconverted men. It shall not be so with you. Be merciful, as your Father in heaven is merciful.

Thirdly, He requires you to walk humbly with thy God. - Christ says, 'Learn of me, for I am meek and lowly of heart.' If God has covered all your black sins - rebellions - backslidings - out-breakings; then never open your mouth except in humble praise. God requires this at your hand. Walk with God, and walk humbly.

October *seventeenth*

True divine peace

*Therefore being justified by faith, we have peace with God
through our Lord Jesus Christ.*
Romans 5 v 1

Justified by faith we have peace with God - not peace with ourselves - not peace with the world, with sin, with Satan, but peace with God. True divine peace is to be f ound only in believing - only in keeping fast hold of Christ. If you let Him go, you let go your righteousness; for this is His name. You are then without righteousness - without a covering from the wrath of God - without a way to the Father. The law will again condemn you; God's frown will again overshadow you; you will again have terrors of conscience. Hold Him then, and do not let Him go. Whatever you let go, let not Christ go; for He is our peace - not in knowledge - not in feeling - but trust in Him alone.

The blood of Jesus

But if we walk in the light, as he is in the light, we have
fellowship one with another, and the blood of Jesus Christ
his Son cleanseth us from all sin.
I John 1 v 7

You need the blood of Jesus as much as at the first. You never can stand before God in yourself. You must go again and again to be washed; even on your dying bed you must hide under Jehovah, our Righteousness. You must also lean upon Jesus. He alone can overcome in you. Keep nearer and nearer every day.

The essence of Christiainity

To whom God would make known what is the riches of the
glory of this mystery among the Gentiles; which is
Christ in you, the hope of glory:
Colossians 1 v 27

Christ in you, means embraced by faith as our righteousness and strength; and this is the sure ground upon which we hope for glory. In this sense it appears to be used, 'That Christ may dwell in your hearts by faith.' (Ephesians 3 v.17.). When a sinner's heart is opened by the Holy Spirit, when the beauty and excellence of the Saviour is shown to him, the heart inwardly embraces and cleaves to Christ. Every new discovery of Christ to the soul renews this act of inward cleaving to the Lord Jesus. Every reproach, every temptation, every fall into sin, every bereavement, makes the soul more really, firmly, and fully embrace the Lord Jesus; and so, by continual faith, Christ may be said to dwell in the heart; as in Ephesians 3 v. 17, 'That Christ may dwell in your heart by faith.' Christ thus embraced is the hope of glory. It is this constant abiding faith - this close embracing of Christ as all our righteousness - it is this which gives a calm, sweet, full, peaceful hope of glory. The soul that can say Christ is mine, can also say, Glory is mine; for we need nothing but Christ to shelter us in the judgement day. Can you say that Christ is thus in you the hope of glory? If you have not got Christ, you have no good hope of glory.

October *twentieth*

The sinner's friend

In all their affliction he was afflicted, and the angel of his presence saved them: in his love and in his pity he redeemed them; and he bare them, and carried them all the days of old.
Isaiah 63 v 9

Dear friend, do you feel that Jesus is your Surety and Elder Brother? Then remember that, by reason of His real Divinity, He is now by your bedside, afflicted in all your afflictions, touched with a feeling of your infirmities, and able to save you to the uttermost. He is as really beside you as He was beside Mary when she sat at His feet. Tell Him all your sorrows, all your doubts and anxieties. He has a willing ear. Oh, what a friend is Jesus! the sinner's friend. What an open ear He has for all the wants, doubts, difficulties of His dying disciples. You know how it is with a kind mother, even though a worldly person. In a time of danger she clasps her children to her breast. In a time of health she may often let them wander out of her sight, but in hours of sickness she will watch beside their bed. Much more will Jesus watch over you.

October *twenty-first*

Arrange beforehand

And it came to pass, that, as he was praying in a certain place, when he ceased, one of his disciples said unto him, Lord, teach us to pray, as John also taught his disciples.
Luke 11 v 1

Pray to be taught to pray. Do not be content with old forms that flow from the lips only. Most Christians have need to cast their formal prayers away, to be taught to cry, Abba. Arrange beforehand what you have to pray for. Do not forget confession of sin, nor thanksgiving. Pray to get your closed lips opened in intercession - embrace the whole world and carry it within the vail.

182

He is precious

Jesus Christ the same yesterday, and to day, and for ever.
Hebrews 13 v 8

How sweet, that Jesus ever liveth. He is the same yesterday, and to-day, and forever. You will never find Jesus so precious as when the world is one vast howling wilderness. Then He is like a rose blooming in the midst of the desolation - a rock rising above the storm. The Bible, too, is more full of meaning. Have you ever prayed over that verse, 'He doth not afflict willingly?' O precious book, that conveys such a message to the mourner's dwelling! And does not trial bring more meaning out of that verse, 'We know that all things work together for good to them that love God, to them who are called according to his purpose'? The Bible is like the leaves of the lemon tree; the more you bruise and wring them the sweeter the fragrance. 'Is any afflicted? -let him pray.' Do you not find that prayer is sweeter now. The soul finds vent for its feeling toward God. 'Call upon me in the day of trouble - I will deliver thee, and thou shalt glorify me.'

Blessings out of buffetings

These things I have spoken unto you, that in me ye might have peace.
In the world ye shall have tribulation: but be of good cheer;
I have overcome the world.
John 16 v 33

It is one of the laws of Christ's kingdom, 'We must, through much tribulation, enter into the kingdom of God.' We must not reckon upon a smooth road to glory, but it will be a short one. How glad I am that you have 'received the word in much affliction, with joy of the Holy Ghost.' Cleave closely to Jesus, that you may not have to say in a little, 'O that I had affliction back again to quicken me in prayer, and make me lie at His feet.'

Trials make the promise sweet,
Trials give new life to prayer;
Trials bring me to His feet,
Lay me low and keep me there.

October *twenty-fourth*

This is happiness

Let your conversation be without covetousness; and be
content with such things as ye have: for he hath said,
I will never leave thee, nor forsake thee.
Hebrews 13 v 5

You may take these words, and apply them to God the Father. And here they come to be very much the words God gave to Abraham: He said, 'Fear not, Abram; I am thy shield and thy exceeding great reward.' He had returned from the slaughter of Chederlaomer, and of the kings that were with him. The king of Sodom came out to meet him, and said unto him. 'Give me the persons, and take the goods to thyself.' But Abraham said, 'I have lift up mine hand unto the Lord, the most high God, the possessor of heaven and earth, that I will not take from a thread even to a shoe latchet, and that I will not take any thing that is thine, lest thou shouldest say, I have made Abram rich.' And immediately after, God appeared to him, and said: 'Fear not, Abram; I am thy shield, and thy exceeding great reward.' This is what Asaph felt. He says, in the seventy-third Psalm, 'My flesh and my heart faileth; but God is the strength of my heart, and my portion for ever. Ah, brethren, this is a sweet word to a poor soul who is mourning over the broken pots at his feet. This is a sweet word to those of you who are bereft - who have left houses and lands - 'I will never leave thee, nor forsake thee.' This may be a sweet word to those of you who are mourning over the dead. O brethren! is this your portion? Can you look up to a three-one God, - Father, Son and Spirit, standing on these broken shreds at your feet, and say, 'Thou wilt never leave me, not forsake me'? This is happiness. Well, well, did the Lord say, 'Mary hath chosen that good part which shall never be taken away from her.' Ah, poor souls, that have chosen the portion that will be taken from you. Ah, brethren! be you wiser.

October *twenty-fifth*

Deep rooted faith

I held him, and would not let him go....
Song of Solomon 3 v 4

The only way to hold fast is to believe more and more. Get a larger acquaintance with Christ - with His person, work, and character. Every page of the Gospel unfolds a new feature in His character -

every line of the Epistles discloses new depths of His work. Get more faith, and you will get a firmer hold. A plant that has got a single root may be easily torn up by the hand, or crushed by the foot of the wild beast, or blown down by the wind; but a plant that has a thousand roots struck down into the ground can stand. Faith is like the root - many believe a little concerning Christ - one fact. Every new truth concerning Jesus, is a new root struck downwards. Believe more intensely. A root may be in a right direction, but, not striking deep, it is easily torn up. Pray for deep rooted faith. Pray to be stablished, strengthened, settled. Take a long intense look at Jesus - often, often. If you wanted to know a man again, and he was going away, you would take an intense look at his face. Look then at Jesus - deeply, intensely - till every feature is graven on your heart. Thomas Scott overcame the fear of death by looking intensely at his dead child, who had died in the Lord.

October twenty-sixth

Love divine

> *But God commendeth his love toward us, in that while*
> *we were yet sinners, Christ died for us.*
> Romans 5 v 8

He loved us! He came into the world 'to save sinners, of whom I am chief'. Had He loved one as glorious as Himself, we would not have wondered. Had He loved the holy angels, that reflected His pure, bright image, we would not have wondered. Had He loved the lovely among the sons of men - the amiable, the gentle, the kind, the rich, the great, the noble - it would not have been so great a wonder. But, ah! He loved sinners - the vilest sinners - the poorest, meanest, guiltiest wretches that crawl upon the ground. Manasseh, who murdered his own children, was one whom he loved; Zaccheus, the grey-haired swindler, was another; blaspheming Paul was a third; the wanton of Samaria was another; the dying thief was another; and the lascivious Corinthians were more. 'And such were some of you.' We were black as hell when he looked on us - we were hell-worthy, under His Father's wrath and curse - and yet He loved us, and said: I will die for them. 'Thou hast loved me out of the pit of corruption', each saved one can say. Oh, brethren! this is strange love: He that was so great, and lovely, and pure, chose us, who were mean and filthy with sin, that He might wash and purify, and present us to Himself. This love passeth knowledge!

October *twenty-seventh*

Love everything that is Christ's

I hate vain thoughts: but thy law do I love.
Psalm 119 v 113

We love everything that is Christ's. We love His Word. It is better to us than thousands of gold and silver. 'O how we love His law - it is our study all the day.' We love His house. It is our trysting-place with Christ, where He meets with us and communes with us from off the mercy-seat. We love His table. It is His banqueting house, where His banner over us is love, where He looses our bonds, and anoints our eyes, and makes our hearts burn with holy joy. We love His people, because they are His, members of His own body, washed in His blood, filled with His Spirit, our brothers and sisters for eternity. And we love the Lord's Day, because it is His. Every hour of it is dear to us - sweeter than honey, more precious than gold. It is the day He rose for our justification. It reminds us of His love, and His finished work, and His rest. And we may boldly say that that man does not love the Lord Jesus who does not love the entire Lord's Day.

October *twenty-eighth*

A great privilege

For if, when we were enemies, we were reconciled to God by the death of his Son, much more, being reconciled, we shall be saved by his life.
Romans 5 v 10

When we are brought to see the reconciled face of God in peace, that is a great privilege. But how can we look upon that face, reconciling and reconciled, and not love Him who hath so loved us? Love begets love. We can hardly keep from esteeming those on earth who really love us, however worthless they may be. But, ah! my friends, when we are convinced that God loves us, and convinced in such a way as by the giving up of His Son for us all, how can we but love Him in whom are all excellencies - everything to call forth love?

Why God waits

Again I say unto you, That if two of you shall agree on earth as
touching any thing that they shall ask, it shall be done for them of
my Father which is in heaven.
Matthew 18 v 19

Many Christians neglect this promise. In the Acts, we find that when the apostles and disciples were praying together, 'the place was shaken where they were assembled together, and they were all filled with the Holy Ghost, and they spake the Word of God with boldness.' Oh, how often and how long have we despised this way of obtaining the outpouring of the Spirit! Do not some persons speak slightingly of united prayer? Here is one reason why God commands the clouds that they rain no rain on us. He waits till we seek Him together, and then He will open the windows of heaven and pour down a blessing.

The chief beauty in Christ

I am the good shepherd: the good shepherd giveth
his life for the sheep.
John 10 v 11

This is the chief beauty in Christ. The wounds that marred His fair body make Him altogether lovely in a needy sinner's eye. All that are now and ever shall be the sheep of Christ, were once condemned to die. The wrath of God abode upon them. They were ready to drop into the burning lake. Jesus had compassion upon them, left His Father's bosom, emptied Himself, became a worm and no man, and died under the sins of many. 'While we were yet sinners, Christ died for us.' This is the grace of the Lord Jesus. Every one in the flock can say, 'He loved me, and gave Himself for me.'

October *thirty-first*

Two heavens

What man of you, having an hundred sheep, if he lose one of them,
doth not leave the ninety and nine in the wilderness, and go after
that which is lost, until he find it?
Luke 15 v 4

Go brother, leaving the ninety-nine, go after the one sheep that was lost. Leave your home, your comforts, your bed, your ease, your all, to feed lost souls. The Lord of Glory left heaven for this; it is enough for the disciple to be as his Master. It is said of Alleine, that 'he was infinitely and insatiably greedy of the conversion of souls.' Rutherford wrote to his dear people, 'My Witness is above, that your heaven would be two heavens to me, and the salvation of you all as two salvations to me.' The Lord give you this heavenly compassion for this people. Do not be satisfied without conversion.

The Enquiry Room at St. Peter's.

November

> "
>
> *His preaching was impressive, for his life applied it. His everyday demeanour exemplified and adorned his doctrine.*
>
> "

A WRITER IN THE PRESBYTERIAN REVIEW

November *first*

The true happiness of a believer

As the hart panteth after the water brooks, so panteth
my soul after thee, O God.
Psalm 42 v 1

Hear David - 'As the hart panteth after the water brooks, so panteth my soul after thee, O God. My soul thirsteth for God, for the living God: when shall I come and appear before God?' He panteth not after the gifts of God - not His favours or comforts - but after Himself. A believer longs after God - to come into His presence - to feel His love - to feel near to Him in secret - to feel in the crowd that He is nearer than all the creatures. Ah! dear brethren, have you ever tasted this blessedness? There is greater rest and solace to be found in the presence of God for one hour, than in an eternity of the presence of man. To be in His presence - under His love - under His eye - is heaven, wherever it be. God can make you happy in any circumstances. Without Him, nothing can.

November *second*

Busy

I must work the works of him that sent me, while it is day:
the night cometh, when no man can work.
John 9 v 4

Our Lord went about continually doing good; He made it His meat and drink. 'Daily in the temple.' So should we. Satan is busy at all times - he does not stand upon ceremony - he does not keep himself to Sabbath days or canonical hours. Death is busy. Men are dying while we are sleeping. About fifty die every minute; nearly one every second entering into an unchangeable world! The Spirit of God is busy. Blessed be God He hath cast our lot in times when there is the moving of the Great Spirit among the dry bones. Shall ministers then be idle, or stand upon ceremony? O that God would baptise us this day with the Holy Ghost and with fire, that we might be all changed as into a flame of fire, preaching and building up Christ's Church till our latest, our dying hour.

Justified

And by him all that believe are justified from all things, from which
ye could not be justified by the law of Moses.
Acts 13 v 39

Once Jesus was unjustified - once there were sins laid to His charge - the sins of many. It was this that occasioned His agony in the garden - on the cross. His only comfort was, 'He is near that justifieth me.' He knew the time would be short. But now the wrath of God has all fallen upon Him. The thunder clouds of God's anger have spent all their lightnings on His head. The vials of God's wrath have poured out their last drops upon Him. He is now justified from all the sins that were laid upon Him. He has left them with the grave-clothes. His fellow men and devils laid all sins to His charge; He was silent. Do you believe this record concerning the Son? Do you cleave to Jesus as yours? Then you have fellowship with Him in His justification. You are as much justified as Christ is. There is as little guilt lying upon you as there is upon Christ. The vials of wrath have not another drop for Christ, nor another drop for you. You are justified from all things.

A living picture

After the same manner also he took the cup, when he had supped,
saying, This cup is the new testament in my blood: this do ye,
as oft as ye drink it, in remembrance of me.
I Corinthians 11 v 25

You cannot look at Him on the cross as the disciples did - you cannot see Him shedding His blood that the blood of sinners might not be shed. Yet still, if God spare us, you may see bread broken and wine poured out - a living picture of the dying Saviour. His sufferings are all past. And how is it that you do not enjoy peace? It is because you do not consider. 'Israel doth not know, my people doth not consider.' Consider - has Jesus died in the stead of guilty sinners, and do you heartily consent to take Jesus to be the man in your stead? Then, you do not need to die. O happy believer, rejoice evermore. Live within sight of Calvary, and you will live within sight of glory; and, O rejoice in the happy ordinance that sets a broken Saviour so plainly before you.

November *fifth*

Chosen

According as he hath chosen us in him before the foundation of the
world, that we should be holy and without blame before him in love:
Ephesians 1 v 4

So brethren, it was before the foundation of the world that Christ chose His own; when there was neither sun nor moon; when there was neither sea nor land - it was from the beginning. Ah, He might well say, you have not chosen me. It was before man loved man, or angel loved angel, that Christ chose His own. Now, I know the meaning of Paul when he says, That you may be able to know the length and breadth, the height and the depth of the love of Christ, which passeth knowledge. Now, I am not surprised at the death of Christ! It was a love so great that it broke over the banks that held it in; a love that broke over a Calvary and a Gethsemane. O brethren! do you know this love

November *sixth*

Retirement

And he said unto them, Come ye yourselves apart
into a desert place, and rest a while.
Mark 6 v 31

I am persuaded that I have been brought into retirement to teach me the value and need of prayer. Alas! I have not estimated aright the value of near access unto God. It is not the mere daily routine of praying for certain things that will obtain the blessing. But there must be the need within - the real filial asking of God the things which we need, and which He delights to give. We must study prayer more.

November *seventh*

Separation better than strife

And Abram said unto Lot, Let there be no strife, I pray thee, between
me and thee, and between my herdmen and thy herdmen; for we be
brethren. Is not the whole land before thee? separate thyself, I pray
thee, from me: if thou wilt take the left hand, then I will go to the
right; or if thou depart to the right hand, then I will go to the left.
Genesis 13 vs 8-9

braham yields the choice to Lot. Brethren, this is what it is to be a Christian, this is what Christ did. Do you remember the command to resist not evil? 'But I say unto you, that ye resist not evil: but whosoever shall smite thee on thy right cheek, turn to him the other also.' (Matthew 5 v. 39). Now, many of you do not know the meaning of this; I have been asked its meaning often; Abraham was smitten on the one cheek, and he turned the other also. See also I Corinthians 6 v. 7 - 'Now therefore there is utterly a fault among you, because ye go to law one with another. Why do ye not rather take wrong? why do ye not rather suffer yourselves to be defrauded?' You will see an example of the same thing in chapter 9 v. 19 - 'For although I be free from all men, yet have I made myself servant unto all, that I might gain the more.' My dear brethren, this is exactly what Abraham did, he suffered himself to be defrauded, he suffered himself to be a servant, that he might gain Lot. This was what Christ did Himself. When they smote Him on the one cheek He turned the other also. Ah, brethren, you know little of the love of Christ, if this is not in your heart. There is a great mistake, I observe, in our day; people think that to be a Christian, is to have certain doctrines in the head - to be a Calvinist; but remember, that to be a Christian, is to have Christ in you. Abraham did not say, I will have it, for it is my right to have it. No! but he said, 'Let us separate; if you go to the right hand, I will go to the left.' Ah! this is to be a Christian. It is not words that will make a Christian. It is not views that will make a Christian. It is this, and this alone.

November *eighth*

Only believe

And we know that all things work together for good to them that love
God, to them who are the called according to his purpose.
Romans 8 v 28

Y ou remember Jacob said, when they wanted to take Benjamin away from him, 'All these things are against me.' But in a little while he saw that 'all these things were working together for good to him.' In a little while all his lost children were restored to him, and he and his seed preserved from famine. So will it be with you. If at any time unbelief steals over your heart - if you lose sight of Jesus, our Passover sacrificed for us - if you forget the hand of the all-tender gracious Father of Jesus and of your soul - you will be crying out, all these things are against me. But ah! how soon you will find that everyting in your history, except sin, has been for you. Every wave of trouble has been wafting you to the sunny shores of a sinless eternity. Only believe. Give unlimited credit to our God.

November *ninth*

The same joy

And not only so, but we also joy in God through our Lord Jesus Christ, by whom we have now received the atonement.

Romans 5 v 11

No joy is like the Divine joy. It is infinite, full, eternal, pure unmingled joy. It is light, without any cloud to darken it - it is calm, without any breath to ruffle it. Clouds and darkness are round about Him - storms and fire go before Him; but within, all is peace ineffable, unchangeable. Believers in some measure share in this joy. We might mention some of the elements of God's joy. First, all things happen according to the good pleasure of His will. He has foreordained whatsoever comes to pass. Nothing comes unprepared upon God. Many things are hateful in His sight, yet, looking on the whole, he can delight in all. If you have come to Christ, you will have some drops of His joy. You can look upon all events with a calm, holy joy, knowing that your Father's will and purposes alone shall stand. Second, the conversion of souls. There is joy in the presence of the angels of God over one sinner repenting, more than over ninety-nine who need no repentance. I have no doubt that this is one of the great elements of His joy - seeing souls brought into His favour. God loves to save; He delighteth in mercy; He delights when He can be a just God and a Saviour. If you are come to Christ, you will have the same joy.

The prunings of the Father

Every branch in me that beareth not fruit he taketh away:
and every branch that beareth fruit, he purgeth it, that it
may bring forth more fruit.
John 15 v 2

John experienced many wonderful dealings of God. He experienced many of the prunings of the Father. He was a fruitful branch, and the Father pruned him that he might bring forth more fruit. When he was very old, he was banished to Patmos, an island in the Aegean Sea, and, it is supposed, made a slave in the mines there. He was a companion in tribulation; but he had many sweet shinings of the Father's love to his soul. He had sweet revelations of Christ in the time of his affliction; and he was joyfully delivered out of all his troubles. He experienced peculiarly the fatherly dealings of God. And so may you do, believer. Look where John looked - believe as John believed - and, like him, you will find that you have a Father in heaven, who will care for you, who will correct you in measure, who will stay His rough wind in the day of His east wind, who will preserve you unto His heavenly kingdom.

Comfort for Christians

But he knoweth the way that I take: when he hath tried me,
I shall come forth as gold.
Job 23 v 10

This is precious comfort. There will be an end of your affliction. Christians must have 'great tribulation,' but they come out of it. We must carry the cross, but only for a moment, then comes the crown. I remember one child of God's saying, that if it were God's will that she should remain in trials a thousand years, she could not but delight in His will. But this is not asked of us: we are only called 'to suffer a while.' There is a set time for putting into the furnace, and a set time for taking out of the furnace. There is a time for pruning the branches of the vine, and there is a time when the husbandman lays aside the pruning hook. Let us wait His time - 'he that believeth shall not make haste.' God's time is the best time. But shall we come out the same as we went in? Ah! no, 'we shall come out like gold.' It is this that sweetens the bitterest cup; this brings a rainbow of promise over the darkest cloud. Affliction will certainly purify a believer. How boldly he says it, 'I shall come out like gold.' Ah, how much dross there is in every one of you, dear believers, and in your pastor! 'When I would do good evil is present with me.' Oh, that all the dross may be left behind in the furnace! What imperfection, what sin, mingles with all we have ever done! But are we really fruit-bearing branches of the true vine? Then it is certain that when we are pruned we shall bear more fruit. We shall come out like gold. We shall shine more purely as 'a diadem in the hand of our God.' We shall become purer vessels to hold the sweet smelling incense of praise and prayer. We shall become holy golden vessels for the Master's use in time and in eternity.

November *twelfth*

All love's excelling

There is no fear in love; but perfect love casteth out fear: because fear hath torment. He that feareth is not made perfect in love.
I John 4 v 18

The love here spoken of is not our love to God, but His love to us; for it is called perfect love. All that is ours is imperfect. When we have done all, we must say, 'We are unprofitable servants.' Sin mingles with all we think and do. It were no comfort to tell us, that if we would love God perfectly, it would cast out fear; for how can we work that love into our souls? It is the Father's love to us that casteth out fear. He is the Perfect One. All His works are perfect. He can do nothing but what is perfect. His knowledge is perfect knowledge; His wrath is perfect wrath; His love is perfect love. It is this perfect love which casteth out fear. Just as the sunbeams cast out darkness wherever they fall, so does this love cast our fear.

The best argument of all

Who is this that cometh out of the wilderness like pillars
of smoke, perfumed with myrrh and frankincense,
with all powders of the merchant?
Song of Solomon 3 v 6

The holiness of the believer is like the most precious perfume. When a holy believer goes through the world, filled with the Spirit, made more than conqueror, the fragrance fills the room, " 'tis as if an angel shook his wings." If the world were full of believers it would be like a bed of spices; but, oh! how few believers carry much of the odour of heaven along with them? How many you might be the means of saving, if you lived a holy, consistent life - if you were evidently a sacrifice bound upon God's altar? Wives might thus, without the word, win their husbands, when they see your chaste conversation coupled with fear; parents might in this way save their children, when they saw you holy and happy; children have often thus saved their parents. Servants, adorn the doctrine of God your Saviour in all things; let your light shine before men. The poorest can do this as well as the richest, the youngest as well as the oldest. Oh, there is no argument like a holy life.

The believer's tears and triumphs

O wretched man that I am! who shall deliver me from the body of this
death? I thank God through Jesus Christ our Lord. So then with the
mind I myself serve the law of God; but with the flesh the law of sin.
Romans 7 vs 24-25

There is nobody in this world so happy as a believer. He has come to Jesus, and found rest. He has the pardon of all his sins in Christ. He has near approach to God as a child. He has the Holy Spirit dwelling in Him. He has the hope of glory. In the most awful times he can be calm, for he feels that God is with him. Still there are times when he cries, O wretched man! When he feels the plague of his own heart - when he feels the thorn in the flesh - when his wicked heart is discovered in all its fearful malignity. Ah, then he lies down, crying, O wretched man that I am! One reason of this wretchedness is, that sin, discovered in the heart, takes away the sense of forgiveness. Guilt comes upon the conscience, and a dark cloud covers the soul. How can I ever go back to Christ? he cries. Alas! I have sinned away my Saviour. Another reason is, the loathsomeness of sin. It is felt like a viper in the heart. A natural man is often miserable from his sin, but he never feels its loathsomeness; but to the new creature it is vile indeed. Ah! brethren, do you know anything of a believer's wretchedness? If you do not, you will never know his joy. If you know not a believer's tears and groans, you will never know his song of victory.

November *fifteenth*

The cure for a cold heart

We love him, because he first loved us.
I John 4 v 19

When a poor sinner cleaves to Jesus, and finds the forgiving love of God, he cannot but love God back again. When the prodigal returned home, and felt his father's arms around his neck, then did he feel the gushings of affection toward his father. When the summer sun shines full down upon the sea, it draws the vapours upward to the sky. So when, the sunbeams of the Sun of Righteousness fall upon the soul, they draw forth the constant risings of love to Him in return.

Some of you are longing to be able to love God. Come into His love, then. Consent to be loved by Him, though worthless in yourself. It is better to be loved by Him than to love, and it is the only way to learn to love Him. When the light of the sun falls upon the moon, it finds the moon dark and unlovely; but the moon reflects the light, and casts it back again. So let the love of God shine into your breast, and you will cast it back again. The love of Christ constraineth us. 'We love Him, because he first loved us.' The only cure for a cold heart is to look at the heart of Jesus.

The world crucified to the believer

But God forbid that I should glory, save in the cross of our Lord Jesus Christ, by whom the world is crucified unto me, and I unto the world.
Galatians 6 v 14

The world is crucified unto me, and I unto the world. - 'If any man be in Christ Jesus, he is a new creature.' When the blind beggar of Jericho got his eyes opened by the Lord, this world was all changed to him, and he to the world. So it was with Paul. No sooner did he rise from his knees, with the peace of Jesus in his heart, than the world got its death blow in his eyes. As he hurried over the smooth stones of the streets of Damascus, or looked down from the flat roof of his house upon the lovely gardens on the banks of the Abana, the world and all its dazzling show seemed to his eye a poor, shrivelled, crucified thing. Once it was his all. Once its soft and slippery flatteries were pleasant as music to his ear. Riches, beauty, pleasure, all that the natural eye admires, his heart was once set upon; but the moment he believed on Jesus all these began to die. True, they were not dead, but they were nailed to a cross. They no more had that living attraction for him they once had; and now every day they began to lose their power. As a dying man on the cross grows weaker and weaker every moment, while his heart's blood trickles from the deep gashes in his hands and feet, so the world, that was once his all, began to lose every moment its attractive power. He tasted so much sweetness in Christ, in pardon, access to God, the smile of God, the indwelling Spirit, that the world became every day a more tasteless world to him.

The believer's self watch

Take heed unto thyself, and unto the doctrine; continue in them: for in doing this thou shalt both save thyself, and them that hear thee.
I Timothy 4 v 16

Your own soul is your first and greatest care. You know a sound body alone can work with power; much more a healthy soul. Keep a clear conscience, through the blood of the Lamb. Keep up close communion with God. Study likeness to Him in all things.

November *eighteenth*

The heart of the Father

And all that dwell upon the earth shall worship him, whose
names are not written in the book of life of the Lamb slain
from the foundation of the world.
Revelation 13 v 8

O brethren, could I lift you away to the eternity that is past: - could I bring you into the council of the Eternal Three; and as it was once said 'Let us make man;' could I let you hear the word, 'Let us save man;' - could I show you how God from all eternity designed His Son to undertake for poor sinners; how it was the very plan and the bottommost desire of the heart of the Father that Jesus should come into the world and do and die in the stead of sinners; how the Holy Spirit breathed sweetest incense, and dropped like holiest oil upon the head of the descending Saviour; - could I show you the intense interest with which the eye of God followed Jesus through His whole course of sorrow, and suffering, and death; - could I show you the anxious haste with which God rolled away the stone from the sepulchre while it was yet dark, for He would not leave His soul in hell, neither suffer His Holy One to see corruption; - could I show you the ecstasies of love and joy that beat in the bosom of the infinite God when Jesus ascended to His Father and our Father; how He welcomed Him with a fullness of kindness and grace which God alone could give and God alone could receive, saying, 'Thou art my Son, this day have I begotten thee; Thou art indeed worthy to be called my Son; never till this day wast Thou so worthy to be called mine; Thy throne, O God, is for ever and ever; Sit thou on my right hand until I make thine enemies thy footstool.' - O sinner, will you ever doubt any more whether God the Father be seeking Thy salvation - whether the heart of Christ and of His Father be the same in this one grand controversy O believer, consider this Apostle of God - meditate on these things - look and look again, until your peace be like a river, and your righteousness like the waves of the sea - till the breathing of your soul be, Abba, Father!

Infinitely better

These are they which follow the Lamb whithersoever he goeth.
Revelation 14 v 4

cquaint now thyself with Him. Come to Him; do not rest short of Him. You think it a great thing to know a lively Christian: oh! how infinitely better to know God.

Servants

But he that is greatest among you shall be your servant.
Matthew 23 v 11

Jesus expressly says, 'He that is greatest among you shall be your servant.' The angels that see the face of God, stoop to serve the meanest servants of God. Dear Christians, you often pray, 'Thy will be done on earth as it is in heaven.' If you mean anything, you mean that you may serve God as the angels do. If you would be like them, become a ministering spirit.

The eye of faith

Wherefore, holy brethren, partakers of the heavenly calling, consider the Apostle and High Priest of our profession, Christ Jesus.
Hebrews 3 v 1

When Christ ascended from the Mount of Olives, and passed through these heavens, carrying His bloody wounds into the presence of God, and when His disciples had gazed after Him, till a cloud received Him out of their sight - we are told that they returned to Jerusalem with great joy. What! are they joyful at parting with their blessed Master? When he told them He was to leave them, sorrow filled their hearts, and He had to argue with them and comfort them, saying, Let not your be troubled; it is expedient for you that I go away. How, then, are they changed! Jesus has left them, and they are filled with joy. Oh! here is the secret - they knew that Christ was now going into the presence of God for them, that their great High Priest was now entering within the vail to make intercession for them.

Now believer, would you share in the great joy of the disciples? Consider the Apostle and High Priest of our profession, Christ Jesus. He is above yon clouds, and above yon sky. O that you would stand gazing up into heaven, not with the bodily eye, but with the eye of faith. Oh! what a wonderful thing the eye of faith is: it sees beyond the stars, it pierces to the throne of God, and there it looks on the face of Jesus making intercession for us, whom having not seen we love, in whom, though now we see Him not, yet believing we rejoice with joy unspeakable and full of glory.

November *twenty-second*

The perfection of God poured forth

And the Word was made flesh, and dwelt among us,
(and we beheld his glory, the glory as of the only begotten of the
Father) full of grace and truth.
John 1 v 14

Christ did not get more glory by becoming man; but He manifested his glory in a new way. He did not gain one perfection more by becoming man; He had all the perfections of God before. But now these perfections were poured through a human heart. The Almightiness of God now moved in a human arm. The infinite love of God now beat in a human heart. The compassion of God to sinners now glistened in a human eye. God was love before, but Christ was love covered over with flesh. Just as you have seen the sun shining through a coloured window. It is the same sunlight still, and yet it shines with a mellowed lustre. So in Christ dwelt all the fullness of the Godhead bodily. The perfection of the Godhead shone through every pore - through every action, word and look - the same perfections; - they were only shining with a mellowed brightness. The vail of the temple was a type of His flesh; because it covered the bright light of the holiest of all. But just as the bright light of the shecinah often shone through the vail, so did the Godhead of Christ force itself through the heart of the man Christ Jesus.

The secret of victory

And be not drunk with wine, wherein is excess;
but be ye filled with the Spirit;
Ephesians 5 v 18

L et the Holy Spirit fill every chamber of your heart; and so there will be no room for folly, or the world, or Satan or the flesh.

One hour with God

But it is good for me to draw near to God: I have put my trust in the
Lord God, that I may declare all thy works.
Psalm 73 v 28

Y ou will get more knowledge in one hour with God than in all your life spent with man. You will get more holiness from immediate conversing with God than from all other means of grace put together. Indeed, all means are empty vanity, unless you come to God in them.

Spiritual warfare

Dearly beloved, I beseech you as strangers and pilgrims, abstain from
fleshly lusts, which war against the soul.
I Peter 2 v 11

T here can never be peace in the bosom of a believer. There is a peace with God but there is always a constant war with sin.

November *twenty-sixth*

He is mine

My beloved is mine, and I am his: he feedeth among the lilies.
Song of Solomon 2 v 16

In the arms of my faith He is mine. I was once of the world - cold and careless about my soul. God awakened me, and made me feel I was lost. I tried to make myself good - to mend my life; but I found it in vain. I sat down more lost than before. I was then told to believe on the Lord Jesus. So I tried to make myself believe. I read books on faith, and tried to bend my soul to believe, so that I might get to heaven; but still in vain. I found it written, 'Faith is the gift of God.' 'No man can call Jesus Lord, but by the Holy Ghost.' So I sat down more lost than ever. Whilst I was thus helpless, Jesus drew near - His garments dipped in blood. He had waited long at my door, though I knew it not. 'His head was filled with dew, and His locks with the drops of the night.' He had five deep wounds; and He said, 'I died in the stead of sinners; and any sinner may have Me for a Saviour. You are a helpless sinner, will you have Me?' How can I resist Him? He is all I need! I held Him, and would not let Him go.' 'My beloved is mine.'

In the arms of my love He is mine. Once I did not know what people meant by loving Jesus. I always wished to ask how they could love one whom they had never seen, but was answered, 'whom not having seen, we love.' But now that I have hidden in Him - now that I am cleaving to Him - now I feel that I cannot but love Him; and I long to see Him that I may love Him more. Many a time I fall into sin, and that takes away my feeling of safety in Christ. Darkness comes, all is clouded, Christ is away. Still even then I am sick of love. Christ is not light and peace to me; but I follow hard after Him amid the darkness - He is precious to me; and even, though I be in darkness, He is my beloved still.' 'This is my beloved, and this is my friend.'

November *twenty-seventh*

Delay in answered prayer

For the vision is yet for an appointed time, but at the end it shall speak, and not lie: though it tarry, wait for it; because it will surely come, it will not tarry.
Habakkuk 2 v 3

When the merchant sends his shops to distant shores, he does not expect them to come back richly laden in a single day. He has long patience. 'It is good that a man should both hope and quietly wait for the salvation of the Lord.' Perhaps your prayers will come back like the ships of the merchant, all the more heavily laden with blessings, because of the delay.

Here is the victory

O death, where is thy sting? O grave, where is thy victory?
I Corinthians 15 v 55

There is nothing that we naturally shrink back from more than the grave. Ah! it is a fearful thing to leave the company of living men, and lie down in the narrow house, with a shroud for our only clothing, a coffin for our couch, and the worm for our companion. It is humiliating, it is loathsome. But if you are one of Christ's, here is the victory: 'In a moment, in the twinkling of an eye, at the last trump: for the trumpet shall sound, and the dead shall be raised incorruptible, and we shall be changed. For this corruptible must put on incorruption, and this mortal must put on immortality. So when this corruptible shall have put on incorruption, and this mortal shall have put on immortality, then shall be brought to pass the saying that is written, Death is swallowed up in victory. O death, where is thy sting? O grave, where is thy victory? (I Corinthians 15 vs. 52 - 55.)

A divine power

So, as much as in me is, I am ready to preach the gospel to you that are at Rome also.
Romans 1 v 15

Men would laugh at the idea of a poor worm like Paul going to subdue mighty Rome with a few words of his lips; but Paul saw such a divine power in the gospel that he was not ashamed of it. He knew it could break the hardest heart, and bind up the most broken. The learned men of Rome would smile at the words of this babbler; but Paul saw such wisdom in the gospel, that all human wisdom appeared utter folly beside it. The wickedness of Rome reached up to heaven; it was a continual smoke in God's nostrils, a fire that burned all the day. But Paul knew that the righteousness of God could cover the sin of a thousand Romes. He saw it to be so vast, so immense, so free, so surpassing glorious, so divine, that it could flow over and cover the sins of the greatest sinner there.

A *whole Saviour*

And the very God of peace sanctify you wholly; and I pray God your whole spirit and soul and body be preserved blameless unto the coming of our Lord Jesus Christ.
I Thessalonians 5 v 23

Learn the certainty of sanctification. Rutherford said, 'Blessed be God, Christ is a whole Saviour - He not only justifies, but He sanctifies too.' Oh, no, He will not lose the end for which He died - to make you not of this world, while you are in the world. He came to this miserable world, and took stones to polish for His Father's palace. Do you ever think He will leave you unholy? This is the will of the Father, even your sanctification. Jesus died, and the Spirit is sent as the sanctifier. There is much sin between you and God - many temptations - yet you shall be made holy.

December

> "
>
> *Oh, that one could have more of the spirit of Mr. McCheyne, and see again the work of those days.*
>
> "

Dr. F. B. Meyer

ChristVelnifested

Christ manifested

And ye know that he was manifested to take away our sins;
and in him is no sin.
I John 3 v 5

O beloved, if Jesus had not been manifested, you had never been saved. It would have been quite righteous in God to have kept His Son in His own bosom - to have kept that jewel in His own place upon the throne of heaven. God would have been the same lovely God; but we would have lain down in a burning hell. If that Eternal Life which was with the Father - if He had remained in His glory as the Living One - then you and I would have borne our own curse. But he was manifested - 'God was manifest in the flesh - justified in the Spirit - seen of angels - believed on in the world - received up into glory.'

John saw Him - he saw His lovely countenance, he beheld His glory, as the glory of the only begotten of the Father, full of grace and truth. He saw that better Sun veiled with flesh that could not keep the beams of His Godhead from shining through. He saw Him on the Mount, when His face shone like the sun. He saw Him in the garden, when He lay upon the ground. He saw Him on the cross, when He hung between earth and heaven. He looked upon Him - many a time he looked upon His heavenly countenance - his eye met His eye.

He heard Him - heard the voice that said, 'Let there be light!' He heard all His gracious words - His words concerning God and the way of peace. He heard Him say to a sinner, 'Be of good cheer, thy sins are forgiven thee.'

He handled Him - he put his hands in His hands, his arms around His arms, and his head upon His bosom. Perhaps he handled His body when it was taken from the cross - touched the cold clay of Immanuel. O beloved, it is a manifested Christ we declare unto you. It is not the Son in the bosom of the Father - that would never have saved you. It is Jesus manifested in flesh. The Son of God living and dying as man in the stead of sinners; Him we declare unto you.

A day of double blessing

I was in the Spirit on the Lord's day, and heard behind me
a great voice, as of a trumpet.
Revelation 1 v 10

When God instituted the Sabbath in paradise, it is said, 'God blessed the seventh day, and sanctified it:' He not only set it apart as a sacred day, but made it a day of blessing. Again, when the Lord Jesus rose from the dead on the first day of the week before dawn, He revealed Himself the same day to two disciples going to Emmaus, and made their hearts burn within them (Luke 24 v. 13). The same evening He came and stood in the midst of the disciples, and said, 'Peace be unto you;' and He breathed on them and said, 'Receive ye the Holy Ghost' (John 20 v. 19).

Again, after eight days, - that is, the next Lord's day, - Jesus came and stood in the midst, and revealed Himself with unspeakable grace to unbelieving Thomas (John 20 v. 26). It was on the Lord's day also that the Holy Spirit was poured out at Pentecost (Acts 2 v. 1; compare Lev. 23 vs. 15-16). That beginning of all spiritual blessings, that first revival of the Christian Church, was on the Lord's day. It was on the same day that the beloved John, an exile on the sea-girt isle of Patmos, far away from the assembly of the saints, was filled with the Holy Spirit, and received his heavenly revelation. So that in all ages, from the beginning of the world, and in every place where there is a believer, the Sabbath has been a day of double blessing. It is so still, and will be, though all God's enemies should gnash their teeth at it. True, God is a God of free grace, and confines His working to no time or place; but it is equally true, and all the scoffs of the infidel cannot alter it, that it pleases Him to bless His word most on the Lord's day. All God's faithful ministers in every land can bear witness that sinners are converted most frequently on the Lord's day - that Jesus comes in and shows Himself through the lattice of ordinances oftenest on His own day. Saints, like John, are filled with the Spirit on the Lord's day, and enjoy their calmest, deepest views into the eternal world.

December *third*

Joy in religion

Finally, my brethren, rejoice in the Lord.
Philippians 3 v 1

Some people are afraid of anything like joy in religion. They have none themselves, and they do not love to see it in others. Their religion is something like the stars, very high, and very clear, but very cold. When they see tears of anxiety, or tears of joy, they cry out, 'Enthusiasm, enthusiasm!' Well, then, to the law, and to the testimony: 'I sat down under His shadow with great delight.' Is this enthusiasm? O Lord, evermore give us this enthusiasm! May the God of hope fill you with all joy and peace in believing! If it be really in sitting under the shadow of Christ, let there be no bounds to your joy. Oh, if God would but open your eyes, and give you simple, childlike faith, to look to Jesus, to sit under His shadow, then would songs of joy rise from all our dwellings! Rejoice in the Lord always, and again I say, Rejoice!

December *fourth*

The main-spring

For the love of Christ constraineth us; because we thus judge,
that if one died for all, then were all dead.
II Corinthians 5 v 15

That Christ's love to man is here intended, and not our love to the Saviour, is quite obvious, from the explanation which follows, where His dying for all is pointed to as the instance of His love. It was the view of that strange compassion of the Saviour, moving Him to die for His enemies - to bear double for all our sins, to taste death for every man - it was this view which gave Paul the impulse in every labour - which made all suffering light to him, and every commandment not grievous. He 'ran with patience the race that was set before him'. Why? Because, 'looking unto Jesus'. he lived as a man 'crucified unto the world, and the world crucified unto him.' By what means? By looking to the cross of Christ.

As the natural sun in the heavens exercises a mighty and unceasing attractive energy on the planets which circle round it, so did the Sun of Righteousness, which had indeed arisen on Paul with a brightness above that of noon-day, exercise on his mind a continual and an almighty energy, constraining him to live henceforth no more unto himself, but to Him that died for him and rose again. And observe, that it was not temporary, fitful energy, which it exerted over his heart and life, but an abiding and a continued attraction; for he does not say that the love of Christ did once constrain him; or that it shall yet constrain him; of that in times of excitement, in seasons of prayer, or peculiar devotion, the love of Christ was wont to constrain him; but he saith simply, that the love of Christ constraineth him. It is the ever present, ever abiding, ever moving power, which forms the main-spring of all his working; so that, take that away, and his energies are gone, and Paul is become weak as other men.

The presence of Christ

But they constrained him, saying, Abide with us.
Luke 24 v 29

It is the presence of Christ with the soul that gives true peace and true holiness. It is not circumstances, nor ministers, nor place, nor time, but Jesus present. To sit under His shadow, gives great delight. To lean upon the Beloved alone supports his faltering steps. A true believer cannot be satisfied while Christ is away: 'Make haste, my Beloved.' One that is not a wife may be content with other lovers; but the faithful bride longs for the return of her Lord. The ordinances are all cold and barren till he return. Ministers speak, but not to the heart. The companions cannot give rest nor ease. Oh! brethren, do you know what it is to long for Himself - to cry, 'Make haste my beloved.'?

Listen! Jesus is praying

Father, I will that they also, whom thou hast given me, be with me where I am; that they may behold my glory,which thou hast given me: for thou lovedst me before the foundation of the world.
John 17 v 24

Father I will. This is the most wonderful prayer that ever rose from this earth to the throne of God, and this petition is the most wonderful in the prayer. No human lips ever prayed thus before -

'Father I will.' Abraham was the friend of God, and got very near to God in prayer, but he prayed as dust and ashes. 'I have taken upon me to speak unto God that am but dust and ashes.' Jacob had power with God, and prevailed, yet his boldest word was, 'I will not let thee go except thou bless me.' Daniel was a man greatly beloved, and got immediate answer to prayer, and yet he cried to God as a sinner - 'O Lord, hear! O Lord, forgive! O Lord, hearken and do!' Paul was a man who got very near to God, and yet he says, 'I bow my knees to the God and Father of our Lord Jesus Christ.' But when Christ prayed, He cried, 'Father I will.' Why did He pray thus? He was God's fellow. 'Awake O sword against my shepherd, against the man that is my fellow.' He thought it no robbery to be equal with God. It was He that said, 'Let there be light, and there was light.' So now He says, 'Father I will.'

He spoke as the Intercessor with the Father. He felt as if His work were already done. 'I have finished the work which thou gavest me to do.' He felt as if He had already suffered the cross, and now claims the crown. 'Father, I will.' This is the intercession now heard in heaven.

He had one will with the Father. 'I and my Father are one.' One God - one in heart and will. True, He had a holy human soul, and, therefore, a human will; but His human will was one with His divine will. The human string in His heart was tuned to the same string with His divine will.

Learn how surely this prayer will be answered, dear children of God. It is impossible this prayer should be unanswered. It is the will of the Father and of the Son. If Christ wills it, and if the Father wills it, you may be sure nothing can hinder it. If the sheep be in Christ's hand, and in the Father's hand, they shall never perish.

December *seventh*

Sowing and reaping

Cast thy bread upon the waters: for thou shalt
find it after many days.
Ecclesiastes 11 v 1

So it is in giving liberally to the poor out of the love of Jesus. Yet fear not; you shall find a crop after many days. You say, 'If I were a rich Christian, how happy would I be to give!' Now, I just ask you to look at the man sowing seed When he has but little, does he keep back from sowing that little? No; he sows the more anxiously the little he has. Do you the same.

Not yet in heaven

Then answered Peter, and said unto Jesus, Lord,
it is good for us to be here:
Matthew 17 v 4

My friend, you are no believer, if Jesus hath never manifested Himself to your soul in your secret devotions - in the house of prayer, or in the breaking of bread - in so sweet and overpowering a manner, that you have cried out, 'Lord, it is good for me to be here!' Peter must come down again from the mount of glory, and fight the good fight of faith, amid the shame and contumely of a cold and scornful world. And so must every child of God. We are not yet in heaven, the place of open vision and unbroken enjoyment. This is earth, the place of faith, and patience, and heavenward-pointing hope.

The idol God hates most

Ephraim shall say, What have I to do any more with idols?
Hosea 14 v 8

Self-righteousness is the largest idol of the human heart - the idol which man loves most and God hates most. Dearly beloved, you will always be going back to this idol. You are always trying to do something in yourself, to gain God's favour by thinking little of your sin, or by looking to your repentance, tears, prayers; or by looking to your religious exercises, your frames, etc.; or by looking to your graces, the Spirit's work in your heart. Beware of false Christs. Study sanctification to the utmost, but make not a Christ of it. God hates this idol more than all others, because it comes in the place of Christ; it sits on Christ's throne. Just as the worship of the Virgin Mary is the worst of all kinds of idolatry, because it puts her in the place of Christ, so self-righteousness is the idol God hates most, for it sits on the throne of Christ.

Dash it down, dear friends; let it never appear again. It is like Manasseh's carved image in the holiest of all. When Manasseh came home an altered man to Jerusalem, would not his first visit be to the holiest of all? With eager hand he would draw the veil aside; and when he found the carved image, he would dash it down from the throne of God. Go and do like wise. If you feel God's love freely by the righteousness without works, then why would you go back to this grim idol? What have I to do any more with idols?

December *tenth*

Uselessness

> But be ye doers of the word, and not hearers only,
> deceiving your own selves.
> James 1 v.22

It is very striking to see the uselessness of many Christians. Are there none of you who know what it is to be selfish in your Christianity? You have seen a selfish child go into a secret place to enjoy some delicious morsels undisturbed by his companions? So it is with some Christians. They feed upon Christ and forgiveness; but it is alone, and all for themselves. Are there not some of you who can enjoy being a Christian, while your dearest friend is not; and yet you will not speak to him? See here, you have got your work to do. When Christ found you, he said: 'Go, work in my vineyard.' What were you hired for, if it was not to work? What were you saved for, if it was not to spread salvation? What blessed for? Oh! my Christian friends! how little you live as if you were servants of Christ! - how much idle time and idle talk you have! This is not like a good servant. How many things you have to do for yourself! How few for Christ and His people! This is not like a servant.

December *eleventh*

A true mark of grace

> *That I may know him.....*
> Philippians 3 v 10

It is a sure mark of grace to desire more. The High Priest had a beautiful breast plate over his breast, adorned with jewels - make me one of these. He had also a jewel on each shoulder - make me one of these. These were bound with chains of gold; but the believer with chains of love. This is a true mark of grace. If you be contented to remain where you are, without anymore nearness to God, or anymore holiness, this is a clear mark you have got none. Hide me deeper, bind me closer, and carry me more completely.

December *twelfth*

Your name is in the Bible
Unto you, O men, I call; and my voice is to the sons of man.
Proverbs 8 v4

Some of you may be saying, 'If I could see my name in the Bible, then I would believe that Christ wants me to be saved. When Christ called Zaccheus, He said, 'Zaccheus, come down.' He called him by name, and he came down immediately. Now, if Christ would call me by name, I would run to Him immediately.' Now, to you I say, Christ does call you by your name, for He says, 'To you, O men, I call.' Suppose that Christ had written down the names of all the men and women in the world, your name would have been there. Now, instead of writing down every name, He puts them all together in one word, which includes every man and woman, and child - 'Unto you, O men, I call; and my voice is to the sons of man.' So your name is in the Bible. 'Go and preach the Gospel to every creature.'

December *thirteenth*

Change your plan
Looking unto Jesus the author and finisher of our faith;
Hebrews 12 v 2

Some of you have really been brought by God to believe in Jesus. Yet you have no abiding peace, and very little growing in holiness. Why is this? It is because your eye is fixed anywhere but on Christ. You are so busy looking at books, or looking at men, or looking at the world, that you have no time, no heart, for looking at Christ.

No wonder you have little peace and joy in believing. No wonder you live so inconsistent and unholy life. Change your plan. Consider the greatness and glory of Christ, who has undertaken all in the stead of sinners, and you would find it quite impossible to walk in darkness, or to walk in sin. O what mean, despicable thoughts you have of the glorious Immanuel! Lift your eyes from your own bosom, downcast believer - look upon Jesus. It is good to consider your ways, but it is far better to consider Christ.

December *fourteenth*

Love's overflow

Jesus saith unto him, I am the way, the truth, and the life: no man cometh unto the Father but by me.
John 14 v 6

I t is the saying of an old divine, that God often orders it, that when He is in hand with the greatest mercies for us, then we are most of all sinning against Him; which He doth to magnify His love the more.

In the words I have read, we find an example of this. At no time did the heart of Jesus overflow with a tenderer and more sovereign love to His disciples, than when He said 'Let not your heart be troubled.' They were troubled by many things. He had told them that He was going to leave them; He had told them that one should betray Him - that another should deny Him - that they should all be offended because of Him that very night; and perhaps they thought He was going from them in anger. But, whatever the cause of their trouble was, Jesus' bosom was like a vessel full to overflowing, and these words were the overlipping drops of love -'Let not your heart be troubled: ye believe in God, believe also in me.'

December *fifteenth*

Sinking saints

But, when he saw the wind boisterous, he was afraid; and beginning to sink, he cried, saying, Lord, save me.
Matthew 14 v 30

O nce Peter 'walked on the water, to go to Jesus. But when he saw the wind boisterous he was afraid; and beginning to sink, he cried, saying Lord, save me. And immediately Jesus stretched forth his hand, and caught him, and said unto him, O thou of little faith, wherefore didst thou doubt?' Christ has an almighty arm for sinking disciples to cling to. Once two disciples were walking towards a village north of Jerusalem. They talked earnestly together to beguile the way, and they were sad. A stranger drew near, and went with them, And as he went he expounded to them, in all the Scriptures, the things concerning Jesus; in breaking of bread He was revealed to them, and left them exclaiming, 'Did not our hearts burn within us!' So Jesus reveals Himself to His own to this day, and makes the sad bosom burn with holy joy.

December *sixteenth*

The preciousness of Christ to the believer

Unto you therefore which believe he is precious:
I Peter 2 v 7

Consider how precious Christ is. 'In him is life eternal.' In Him there is pardon for the vilest of sinners. In Him there is sweet peace of conscience - peace with God. In Him there is rest for the weary soul - the way to the Father - an open door into the fold of God. In Him there is a fountain of living waters, unsearchable riches, full supplies of grace and truth for weak and weary souls. In Him there is acquittal at the judgement day, and a glorious crown. Oh, should you not leave all for this? Shall a lust, or a pleasure, or a game, or the smile of a friend, keep you from all this? 'Eye hath not seen, nor ear heard, not hath it entered into the heart of man to conceive, the things which God hath prepared for them that love him.'

December *seventeenth*

All precious to Christ

And the stones were according to the names of the children of Israel, twelve, according to their names, like the engravings of a signet, every one with his name, according to the twelve tribes.
Exodus 39 v 14

Observe how precious His people are to Him. There is a variety among the stones - every one is different, yet all are precious. So there is a great variety among Christ's people, yet all are precious to Christ. Some are chosen in infancy, like John the Baptist and

217

Jeremiah, sanctified from the womb. Some are chosen in old age. Some are taken who have committed but little sin, like Martha and Mary. Some who have committed much, like the woman which was a sinner, and the dying thief. Some are taken from a cottage, some from a palace; all are different, yet all jewels in the eyes of the Redeemer.

December *eighteenth*

Selfish children

... ye have not, because ye ask not.
James 4 v 2

When God, in Ezekiel 36 v. 26, promises to give a new heart and a new spirit to Israel - 'I will take away the stony heart out of your flesh, and I will give you an heart of flesh.' - he adds, at verse 37: 'I will yet for this be enquired of by the house of Israel to do it for them;' And when God promises to give to Christ the heathen for His heritage, He only promises it in answer to prayer: 'Ask of me, and I will give thee.' And just so here; when He wishes to give life to these dead carcasses that are lying in the open valley, His word is : 'Prophesy, O son of man, unto the Spirit.'

O believing brethren, what an instrument is this which God hath put into your hands! Prayer moves him that moves the universe. O men of faith and prayer! Israels who wrestle with God, and prevail! Righteous, justified men whose prayers avail much! You may be a little flock, but be you entreated to give the Lord no rest. O pray for the Spirit to 'breathe upon these slain, that they may live!'

And you, selfish Christians, if such a contradiction can exist - you who approach the throne of God only for yourselves, you whose petitions begin and end only for yourselves, who ask no gifts but only for your own peace and joy - go you and learn what this meaneth; 'It is more blessed to give than to receive.' 'Let this mind be in you which was also in Christ Jesus.'

A sight of Christ

And when he had given thanks, he brake it, and said, Take, eat: this is
my body, which is broken for you: this do in remembrance of me.
I Corinthians 11 v 24

An unconverted man cannot remember Christ; for he hath never seen Him, neither known Him. A man who never tasted honey cannot remember the taste of it; so a man who never had a saving taste of the sweetness of the Lord Jesus cannot possibly remember Him. Indeed, there is a kind of remembrance of Christ that any man may have. You may remember the events of His life: that He was born in a stable, that He walked on the Lake of Galilee, that He wept over Jerusalem, that He prayed in Gethsemane, that He died on the cross on Calvary; but even the devils can remember Christ in this way. They remember all His history much more perfectly than we do. Satan has more knowledge of divine things than many doctors of divinity. And lost souls in eternal misery remember Jesus. But, ah! this is not the saving remembrance of Jesus which we have at the Lord's Table.

When a labouring, heavy laden sinner is brought to the feet of Jesus, he finds a joy and peace in believing he never felt before. He gets a discovery of the love of Christ that he never had before; the love of Jesus in coming for the ungodly, and dying for them; the freeness of Christ to every creature, to sinners even the chief, to publicans and sinners, coming to Him; the wisdom and excellency of this way of salvation, the amazing glory and perfection of the righteousness of God. When the Spirit thus takes the veil from the eyes, he gets a sight of Christ which he never will, and never can, forget. This is the spiritual relish and discerning of the Lord's body.

A shield for sinners

Behold, God is my salvation;
Isaiah 12 v 2

If trembling sinners only knew the person who has undertaken to be a Saviour, it would dispel all their fears. He is the brightness of God's glory, and the express image of His person. He is the peerless, matchless Son of God that has undertaken to stand for us. He is the maker of the world, He that sees the end from the beginning. 'By him were all things made.' He made the sun, moon, and stars, He made the solid earth, He upholds all things by the word of His power.

Do you think He would fail in any undertaking? Do you think, if He engages to be a shield for sinners, that He will not be enough to cover them? Oh! be ashamed of your unbelief, and come under this infinite Shield. 'Behold, God is my salvation; I will trust and not be afraid.' Come, trembling soul, under this divine Shield, and you will find divine peace. Come under this Rock, and you will find rest for your weary souls. It matters not what sins you have; if you come to Christ, you shall have peace.

December *twenty-first*

A dying boy's testimony

And when he is come, he will reprove the world of sin, and of righteousness, and of judgement.
John 16 v 8

There is, perhaps, no subject upon which there is greater ignorance than that of the Spirit of God. Most people, in our day, if they answered truly, would say as those twelve men at Ephesus: 'We have not so much as heard whether there be any Holy Ghost' (Acts 19 v. 2). And yet, if ever you are to be saved, you must know him; for it is all His work to bring a poor prisoner to Christ. A little boy, when dying, said: 'Three persons in the Godhead. God the Father made and preserved me; God the Son came into the world and died for me; God the Holy Ghost came into my heart, and made me love God and hate sin.' My dear friends, if you would die happy, you must be able to bear the same dying testimony.

December *twenty-second*

The gospel bell

... a bell and a pomegranate, round about the hem of the robe to minister in; as the Lord commanded Moses.
Exodus 39 v 26

Christians you are priests. Be like Christ in this. Wherever you go, carry a savour of Christ. His name is like ointment poured forth; it is like the vine flourishing, and the pomegranate budding. Let men take knowledge of you, that you have been with Jesus; let it be plain that you come from within the veil; let the smell of your garments be as a field which the Lord hath blessed. Carry a sound of Christ wherever you go. Not a step, Christians, without the sound of the gospel bell. Even in smallest things, be spreading the glad sound. Edwards says, wherever a godly person enters, he is a greater blessing than if the greatest monarch were entering. So be it with you. It appears to me that even the tracts for which you contribute, are like little bells. They are small and despised by some, yet they carry the clear sound of the Gospel wherever they go. What Christian among you would not love to see them multiplied, till every family on the globe should hear the message of mercy? Come, then, to the help of the Lord against the mighty.

December *twenty-third*

Communion with God

Draw nigh to God, and he will draw nigh to you.
James 4 v 8

I ought to spend the best hours of the day in communion with God. It is my noblest and most fruitful employment, and is not to be thrust into any corner. A calm hour with God is worth a whole lifetime with man.

December *twenty-fourth*

The sovereign mercy of Jesus

For verily he took not on him the nature of angels; but he took on him the seed of Abraham. Wherefore in all things it behoved him to be made like unto his brethren, that he might be a merciful and faithful high priest in things pertaining to God, to make reconciliation for the sins of the people. For in that he himself hath suffered being tempted, he is able to succour them that are tempted.
Hebrews 2 vs 16 -18

We read of two great rebellions in the history of the universe - the rebellion of the angels, and the rebellion of man. For in finitely wise and gracious purposes God planned and per- mitted both of these, that out of evil He might bring forth good. The first took place in heaven itself. Pride was the sin by which the angels fell, and, therefore, it is called 'the condemnation of the devil.' 'They kept not their first estate, but left their own habitation.' The next fall took place upon earth. Satan tempted, and man fell - believed the devil rather than God, and so came under the curse -'Thou shalt surely die.' Both of these families came under the same frown - under the same condemnation - both were condemned to the same 'everlasting fire.' But the glorious Son of God resolved, from all eternity, to die for sinners. Now, for which of the two shall He die? Perhaps the angels in heaven would long that He should die for their once brother angels. The angelic nature was higher than that of man. Men had fallen deeper into sin than the rebel angels. Will He not die for angels? Now, here is the answer - 'Verily He took not on Him the nature of angels; but He took on Him the seed of Abraham.' Here is sovereign mercy passing by one of the family and coming to another. Let us wonder and adore the sovereign mercy of Jesus.

December *twenty-fifth*

'Tis the Lord! O Wondrous story'

Behold, a virgin shall be with child, and shall bring forth a son,
and they shall call his name Emmanuel, which being
interpreted is, God with us.
Matthew 1 v 23

In the manger at Bethlehem, there lay a perfect infant, but there also was Jehovah. That mysterious being who rode on an ass's colt, and wept over Jerusalem, was as much a man as you are, and as much God as the Father is. The tears He shed were human tears, yet the love of Jehovah swelled below His mantle. That pale being that hung quivering on the cross was indeed man - it was human blood that flowed from His wounds - but He was as truly God. In being without sin. He was the only one in human form of whom it can be said, he was holy, harmless, undefiled and separate from sinners; the only one on whom God could look down from heaven, and say, 'This is my beloved Son in whom I am well pleased.' Every member of our body and faculty of our mind we have used as the servants of sin. Every member of His body and faculty of His mind were used only as servants to holiness. His mouth was the only human mouth from which none but gracious words ever proceeded. His eye was the only human eye that never shot forth flames of pride, or envy, or lust. His hand was the only human hand that never was stretched forth but in doing good. His heart was the only human heart that was not deceitful above all things and desperately wicked. When Satan came to Him, he found nothing in Him. Now, in these two things it behoved Him to be unlike His brethren, or He could not have been a Saviour at all. In all other things it behoved Him to be made like us. There was no part of our condition that He did not humble Himself unto.

December *twenty-sixth*

A higher place

Therefore leaving the principles of the doctrine of Christ,
let us go on unto perfection;
Hebrews 6 v 1

Unconverted souls are going down into the wilderness to perish there. All Christians are coming up out of it. Sabbath days are like milestones, marking our way; or rather they are like the wells we used to come to at evening. Every real Christian is making progress. If the sheep are on the shoulder of the shepherd, it is always getting nearer the fold. With some the shepherd takes long steps. Dear Christians, you should be advancing, getting higher, nearer to Canaan, riper for glory. In the south of Russia, the country is of vast plains, rising by steppes. Dear friends, you should get on to a higher place, up another step every Sabbath day. In travelling, you never think of making a house in the wilderness. So, dear friends, do not take up your rest here, we are journeying. Let all your endeavours be to get on in your journey.

December *twenty-seventh*

Holiness and your Bible

Sanctify them through thy truth: thy word is truth.
John 17 v 17

Jesus is the author of sanctification; but there are many looking to the wrong airt for it. Now, all comes from the same hand that was nailed to the cross; look to Him for sanctification - His name is Jesus, for He saves from sin. Oh, do any feel faint and weary? Lean on Him, the Beloved: all comes from Jesus. You may as well try to hold up the sun in its course, as to hold up your own goings. Go, then, to Jesus for all you need: learn the means of sanctification - the Word. No holiness without the Bible. I believe God could sanctify without the Word. He made the angels holy without it, and He made Adam holy without it; but He will not do it. 'Sanctify them through thy truth, thy word is truth.' Just like a mother nourishing a child, Jesus takes a soul and nourishes it with the milk of the word. No life without a Bible. It is just the breathings of God's heart - of His affectionate bosom. Oh, yes, if you would walk much with Jesus, you would become like Him. Oh, you would get the heart and likeness of Jesus. There are some believers, and you may know them by their breath that they have been with Emmanuel, the lovely Rose of Sharon. Learn then, that there are no other means of sanctification, and without holiness no man shall see the Lord. Unless you love your Bibles, and feed upon them, you will never stand with the Lamb upon Mount Zion, with the golden harps.

December *twenty-eighth*

High time to wake out of sleep

And that, knowing the time, that now it is high time to awake out of sleep: for now is our salvation nearer than when we believed.
Romans 13 v 11

In these words, Paul tells believers that it is waking time; and I would just tell you, dear friends, the same. It is high time for you to awake out of sleep. There is a condition among Christians which may be called sleeping; like the ten virgins, they slumber and sleep. Ah! I fear there are many sleeping Christians among you. It is waking time, believer. Do you know what o'clock it is? You do not seem to know how near sun-rise it is.

I will now show you what it is to be sleeping Christians. It is to be one that has come to Christ, yet has fallen asleep in sin. Like the Church at Ephesus, they have left their first love. They do not retain that realisation of the Christ's preciousness - that freshness of believing. They have forgotten the fresh grasp of a Saviour. So it is with some among yourselves. You may have seen your sins; yet you have lost that fresh conviction of sin you once felt so deeply. You do not see such a beauty in Jesus. The more we look at Him, just the more we would look again. Earthly things pall upon the taste; but it is not so with things divine. They grow sweeter the oftener you use them. So every time you look at Jesus, He grows more precious. The rose is sweet, yet it loses its smell; but the lovely Rose of Sharon grows sweeter and sweeter. Earthly apples lose their taste; but the apple tree does not so - 'Stay me with the flagons, comfort me with apples, for I am sick of love.' Sleepy Christians, you have lost taste for the apples. Oh! is it not time for you to awake out of sleep? Believer, if you sleep on, you will soon doubt if ever you have come to Christ at all.

December *twenty-ninth*

A mirror of Christ

But we all, with open face beholding as in a glass the glory of the Lord, are changed into the same image from glory to glory even as by the Spirit of the Lord.
II Corinthians 3 v 18

In a mirror you will observe that every feature of the face is reflected - both large and small features. Now our soul should be a mirror of Christ; we should reflect His features; for every grace in Christ, there should be a counterpart grace in us.

December *thirtieth*

Strength

Blessed is the man whose strength is in thee; in whose heart are the ways of them.
Psalm 84 v 5

Remember Jesus for us is all our righteousness before a holy God, and Jesus in us is all our strength in an ungodly world.

December *thirty-first*

My Master's time

Redeeming the time, because the days are evil.
Ephesians 5 v 16

What right have I to steal and abuse my Master's time?
Redeem it,' He is crying to me.

The time is short! - the season near,
When death will us remove,
To leave our friends, however dear,
And all we fondly love!

The time is short! sinners, beware,
Nor trifle time away;
The word of 'great salvation' hear,
'While it is called to-day.'

The time is short! ye rebels, now
To Christ the Lord submit;
To mercy's golden sceptre bow,
And fall at Jesus' feet.

The time is short! ye saints rejoice,
The Lord will quickly come:
Soon shall ye hear the Bridegroom's voice,
To call your spirits home.

The time is short! it swiftly flies,
The hour is just at hand,
When we shall mount above the skies,
And reach Emmanuel's land.

The Gravestone in St. Peter's Churchyard.
"There is still some peculiar fragrance in the air round Robert Murray McCheyne's tomb."

- Dr. Andrew A. Bonar